SHEAR SPIRIT

SHEAR SPIRIT

Ten Fiber Farms, Twenty Patterns, and Miles of Yarn

Joan Tapper
Photography by Gale Zucker

POTTER
CRAFT

New York

Published in the United States by Potter Craft,
an imprint of the Crown Publishing Group,
a division of Random House, Inc., New York.
www.crownpublishing.com
www.pottercraft.com

POTTER CRAFT and colophon is a registered
trademark of Random House, Inc.

Produced by RavenMark
All patterns and illustrations are copyright © 2008
by the individual contributors

Library of Congress Cataloging-in-Publication Data
is available upon request

ISBN: 978-0-307-394033

Printed in China

10 9 8 7 6 5 4 3 2 1

In memory of Anna S. Tapper, who knit beautiful
afghans for her family and friends.

And for the Engler-Zucker guys—
the loves of Gale's life—Dave, Leo & Gabe.

Contents

(Clockwise from top left): Meadowcroft Farm's Seacolors yarns, Ed Cothey and a Bactrian camel at Tregellys Fiber Farm, Icelandic lamb, small wrangler at Victory Ranch, colorful Thirteen Mile Farm yarns, Cas Sochacki and two of his flock at Old Mill Farm, cashmere kid at Goat Knoll Farm, Jay Begay spinning at Lazy J Diamond Ranch, two kids at Kai Ranch, socks knitted with Autumn House Farm yarns.

Introduction

How do you explain a book like *Shear Spirit*? Start at the beginning—with one artistic woman's passion for knitting and her penchant for photographing sheep. This project was Gale Zucker's idea, but early on she, a resident of Connecticut, and Rebecca Davison and Linda Mirabile of RavenMark, in Vermont, joined forces to shape the idea and design. And through a friend, they found me, a writer/editor in California.

And so this book became our cross-country collaboration. How appropriate for a project that embraces crafts traditionally associated with women, a diversity of geographic regions, and creative people who have turned their ideas and dreams into reality (plus all those photogenic animals).

As we visited and interviewed the farmers and ranchers, we noticed obvious differences: Raising sheep on a farm near the coast of Maine is unlike breeding Angora goats on a ranch in inland Texas or alpacas in the high country of New Mexico. But everyone we profiled, it seemed, shared certain characteristics, notably, a love of what they do and a commitment to quality products. It was fascinating and fun to weave together the personal stories, regional histories, craft techniques, and tidbits about rare and heritage animals with a celebration of exciting artistic endeavors.

And it was wonderful to be able to include the original knitting patterns that so beautifully showcase the wool, mohair, cashmere, or alpaca fibers of each farm, as well as the style of each region of the country.

The chapters also reflect the changing seasons and the rhythm of farm routines over a year of research. As we soon learned, breeding, lambing and kidding, shearing, processing fiber, and producing handcrafts all have a special niche in the calendar. It was evident as well that the hard work—and the generosity of time and spirit—take place all year long.

We were lucky to be able to focus on a rich variety of farms and ranches, many of which welcome visitors. At Meadowcroft Farm, in Maine, Nanney Kennedy maintains a sustainable sheep farm and produces sea- and sun-dyed yarn and sweaters. Ed and Jody Cothey have made Tregellys Fiber Farm, in Massachusetts, a veritable geography lesson, with sheep, yaks, camels, and . . . a whole lot more. Autumn House Farm, in Pennsylvania, draws on the Knoxes' family farm tradition. The McDowells of Misty Meadow Icelandics Farm, in Minnesota, specialize in fiber arts and fiber from Icelandic sheep. At Kai Ranch, in Texas, Lisa Shell breeds Angora goats, especially those with colored fleece. Victory Ranch, in New Mexico, is one of the largest alpaca ranches in the Southwest. At Lazy J Diamond Ranch, on the Navajo reservation in Arizona, Jay Begay raises once-endangered Churro sheep and continues his people's traditions. Montana's organic Thirteen Mile Farm, owned by Becky Weed and Dave Tyler, encompasses a wool mill—and a predator-friendly philosophy. In Oregon, at Goat Knoll Farm, Linda Fox and Paul Johnson raise cashmere goats while they keep up their professional careers. And at Old Mill Farm, in California, sheep farming and fiber are just one aspect of the sustainable organic farm run by Cas Sochacki and his family.

We want to thank all these farmers and ranchers for sharing their stories and crafts with us . . . and you, the community of knitters, hand spinners, felters, and crocheters, everyone, in fact, who loves fiber. *Shear Spirit* has, indeed, knit us all closely together.

Face-to-face with a Churro ewe (opposite) at Lazy J Diamond Ranch. Pages 2–3: Darcy Weisner up close and personal with an alpaca at Victory Ranch, which offers fine alpaca yarn. Page 4: the Autumn House Farm flock in a hillside pasture. Page 5: Angora kid at Kai Ranch. Page 6: A merry westerner has a little lamb and wears the Montana Tunic on a ranch near Bozeman.

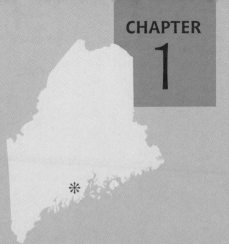

Meadowcroft Farm

Sea, Sun, and Sheep–
They're All Connected

Washington, Maine

Nanney Kennedy and her dog Ollie (opposite) romp in a pasture near her house. Above (clockwise from top left): sea glass button, ewe at Meadowcroft Farm, Seacolors yarn, examining the crimp in a fleece.

On a sunny fall morning in Washington, Maine, Nanney Kennedy is rearranging her fences. As her Border Collie, Ollie, eyes the flock of ewes and lambs, she pulls up stakes, moving the temporary enclosures. It's part of her plan to build the farm's soil and manage the grass that feeds the sheep that grow the wool that yields the yarn that's dyed, woven, and knit into blankets and sweaters . . . you get the idea. And though this description of Nanney's work makes it seem like a child's game, it's actually serious business, a series of inter-connected events that embodies Nanney's concept of sustainability.

"For any kind of production, you need something to exploit," she tells a visitor, "and the beauty of farming in Maine is that we can get seven months of grass." The green stuff is a resource that underpins the way she nurtures her animals, and she never takes it for granted. "At the heart of it," she says, "you can't live off the land. You have to live with it."

Nanney—a nickname for Anne—knows this land well. Born in 1960, she was raised in the area, on Damariscotta Lake. "I'm from right down the watershed," she says, her blue eyes sparkling.

Her eighty-acre Meadowcroft Farm is located on the back side of the Camden Hills, about halfway between Augusta, Maine's capital, and the coast. Her hayfields are edged by the Davis Stream and backed by woods of pine, spruce, poplar, maple, and cherry trees that are beginning to add autumn color to a subtly undulating landscape.

Nanney keeps about a hundred sheep here, mostly homebred versions of the Polwarth breed that she's developed for the kind of fiber she's after: very soft, very fine, with a lively springiness. There are also a Coopworth and a Merino ram, a Jerusalem donkey, three horses, three families of chickens, a Great Pyrenees guard dog called Emma (after her great aunt), and Ollie's two offspring, rambunctious young Border Collies named Hattie and Grace (after Nanney's grandmothers).

An interest in farming and entrepreneurialism apparently runs in her blood. In the nineteenth century, Nanney's great-great-grandfather, Hiram Sibley, owned cattle in California and cornfields in Illinois and was instrumental in developing the Cornell Agricultural School to provide a steady stream of farmers for an expanding nation. (He also started Western Union.) But Nanney got her first taste of agriculture from outside the family.

"As a kid, I spent a tremendous amount of time with my dogs and books, and I used to ride horses," she says, "but I really wanted to learn about farming. When I was thirteen, I was mentored by a woman who was married to the agricultural commissioner. She took me under her wing, and I took care of her horses." It was from this woman that Nanney gained an awareness of the importance of animal care. "She taught me that you take care of your animals before you have your first cup of tea," she adds, "and also passed along the value of healthy food and a healthy lifestyle."

Nanney went on to Bowdoin College and got a BA in the sociology of art, then spent most of a year in New Zealand, learning about grass farming, going to shearing school, and studying farm economy. She later worked as a night shepherd at the Forbes family estate on Naushon Island and lived on Nantucket periodically over five years in the mid-1980s, where she did research on using sheep grazing for conservation management. By 1988, Nanney was married, the mother of two young sons, stepmother to an older daughter, and a graduate student working on a degree in Agriculture and Resource Economics, while she and her husband restored the old house on the farm they'd bought that year.

She also acquired a small flock of sheep from a woman on Maine's North Haven Island. "They were well-naturalized to the climate," Nanney remembers. "I picked them up in December of 1989." In February of the next year, though, her

Nanney (opposite) and freshly dyed yarn. Above: the lily pond.

life changed drastically. The house burned down, obliterating all her academic work. And three years later, her husband walked out, leaving her to raise her sons on her own.

These days the boys are away at school. And Nanney has built a new two-bedroom house with weathered wood siding and terra-cotta trim over a former two-car garage. A side deck that overlooks the fields catches the late afternoon sun. Above the comfortable living room, bay windows frame a view of pasture and woods. Two spinning wheels stand in a corner. One was a gift from an older woman, a hand spinner, who taught Nanney the craft, then gave her the wheel so that she, in turn, could teach others.

Female mentors have played an important role in helping Nanney define her path in life. When she was in college, Nanney spent a few months on a farm with a woman who kept three hundred sheep, learning from her about lambing and helping with chores. Later, a woman artist helped Nanney weave together the various strands of her interests. "For years I'd been doing agricultural production, learning about agronomics," she says. "All the academic models focused me toward producing more products." But raising more sheep can add tremendously to one's costs, she realized. And it wasn't clear how the theoretical business plans connected to her other work, which involved being a hand spinner and dyer on a necessarily small scale. Through the Women's Business Development Corporation in Maine, Nanney acquired a sponsor, "an incredible, wise woman, a potter, who said I was really a craftsperson, not a farmer." Her encouragement and advice made Nanney comfortable with becoming an artisan/entrepreneur.

Nanney's living room is piled with wool: skeins of teal blue and sea green, a huge ring of cinnamon-colored yarn, baskets of cream-colored roving. There are piles and piles of wool everywhere, in eye-catching but delicately varying shades that are the artistic results of Nanney's solar-dyeing process, which takes place on a platform over the foundation of her burned-down house. Also on hand are oversized skeins of naturally colored yarn, commercially spun and waiting to be retied and then dyed.

Nanney talks about her farm and her enterprises with a free-flowing energy, punctuated by frequent hearty laughter. Her conversation bounces rapidly from economics and sociology to craft and creativity. She's full of entrepreneurial ideas and excited by her surroundings and her daily activities.

But it has taken Nanney years to get where she is. "Trying to figure out a business plan took a long time," she says, remembering her first efforts to make money as a hand spinner and dyer. She also sold the meat and skins of her sheep. But in those early days forty hours of work netted her about two hundred dollars. She knew she had to find a better way of making a living within a sustainable framework that also fit in with raising two active boys.

Nanney considered the topography of her farm and what she could breed there, as well as how to "fit it in with my life." And any business had to be economically viable. "Sheep are by nature very sustainable, but it's amazing how little people know about breeding to manage the fiber on an animal," she says. "There's a lot that I do on the farm that are best practices for ecology, but they're expensive as far as sheep are concerned." She adds extra fencing along erodable slopes and waterways to keep the environment pristine and uses double fences in places for predator-friendly coyote control. And she'll forego mechanical haying early in the season, grazing her animals instead, to protect early ground-nesting birds like bobolinks and killdeers.

Checking a lamb (left); Nanney's Polwarth sheep (center) grow fleece with good spinnability (right).

Running the farm is now "part inspiration, part planning—how to move the sheep, how to breed the sheep, how to cull the flock," she says. "I love creating the systems." And she has essentially taken on the entire production process: growing her feed, selling livestock, selling wool, and selling products like sweaters and blankets that create piecework jobs for home knitters and showcase her handspun and hand-dyed yarn. "I've got raw inventory at the mills. I've got wool ready to be dyed. I've got dyed wool ready to be knit. At every stage, I'm ready to go."

The result reflects Nanney's individual blend of art, philosophy, and commerce. "If I can help consumers understand that they can indulge themselves," with a beautiful sweater, for example, "while helping sustain agriculture . . . that's sustainable abundance," she says.

Most days Nanney is up with the sun. She makes a cup of coffee, walks the dogs, and checks the livestock, scanning the ground for signs of coyotes, making sure the fences haven't been compromised, assessing the feed in the pastures. Her flock is divided into three groups, wethers and rams in one, ewes and lambs in two others. They have to be moved every few days to take advantage of the lushness of the grass or to add manure to the field, making it more fertile.

After an hour or so she's back at the house for a toast breakfast and to check her e-mail. On hand to help with the farm chores several months of the year is Ian Stewart, a wiry, bearded former sheep farmer from New Zealand, who swaps his labor for food and shelter, under the auspices of an international program called Willing Workers on Organic Farms. The tasks might include lambing, shearing, worming, or evaluating which animals should be sold to the butcher, for the "one-way ride," as Ian calls it.

When it comes to her breeding program, Nanney is relentless. Her version of Polwarth sheep are the descendents of a fine-wool breed crossed with a breed that has long, soft, lustrous wool, then bred again to a fine-wool animal, producing fiber that meets her standards for soundness, luster, length, weight, and spinnability. She's also aggressive about culling her flock, which is about a hundred animals. "Sometimes it depends on the weather," she says. "If the summer pasture is dry, for example, I sell livestock."

Occasionally, her routine is broken by chance visitors. Often she runs errands, whistling Ollie into the truck to accompany her as she hauls a piece of machinery to be fixed or shops in the nearby town of Rockland. She knows the shopkeepers and stops to chat with old friends.

Working with Ollie to move the flock.

In summer, she also takes time to gather the seawater she uses in her dye vats, sometimes making as many as three or four trips a week to the tidal Damariscotta River estuary. There, in a setting that's quintessential coastal Maine, with dinghies lined up along the town dock and clapboard cottages lining the cove, she backs a sturdy station wagon close to the water. Carrying a dozen five-gallon buckets out onto the pier, she fills them with the clear, cold, briny liquid. Each bucket seems to weigh a ton, but that doesn't faze Nanney, who hoists them, two at a time, back to the waiting vehicle.

"I'm the queen of the watershed," she jokes, adding that when curious onlookers ask what she's doing, "I tell them that I'm the girl in charge of the tides."

Nanney dyes wool all summer, with clean Maine seawater substituting for the chemical salts that are needed to fix the dye in a protein fiber, and the sun (instead of fossil fuels) providing the energy to slowly melt the colors or create color bursts. Her dye tubs are small, each holding about ten skeins, and they sit in four low, glass-topped wooden sheds. The exhausted dyes are recovered and reused. She adapted the setup from parts salvaged from a friend's failed solar business and pieces recovered from her burned-down house.

"I trade temperature for time," she says, meaning that the process takes more hours with just sunshine as a source of heat. Her method of working invariably ties her to nature's rhythms. "My dye season doesn't start before the solstice, and I can go gangbusters for a couple of months. After the equinox, though, the light changes, and I need to ready the animals and the house for a long winter."

Her initial dye lots, years ago, were jars of roving, which she rainbow-dyed indoors in the winter. Later she tried to emulate both the colors and the spirit of chance—and to grow the volume—by adapting her operation to solar energy outdoors.

Most of her colors now come from synthetic aniline carbon-based dyes, though Nanney often uses indigo from her small dyer's garden, which sits beside a lily pond next to her house. Dyeing with indigo appeals to her artistry. When you first pull the yarn out of the vat, she notes, "it's yellow. As the color interacts with oxygen, it turns blue. It's magical!" Her garden also contains madder (which dyes red), woad (for blue), and weld, or ladies' bedstraw (for yellow), among others.

Nanney maintains she's always experimenting: "I might pre-wet the wool and heat it, applying color to get color bursts. The actual time in the vats depends on the strength of the sun."

Bent at the waist in what she calls a "downward dog dye style," Nanney checks her yarn batches frequently, turning the skeins over from time to time until she has the color and effects she wants.

Then she'll loop the skeins onto a frame, each one above a bucket to catch run-off dye. Finally she rinses the yarn three or four times at various temperatures.

The resulting colors are fresh and clear, different each year, depending on the natural fiber colors in her flock and a mystical blend of science, art, nature, and the weather.

"Because the colors change," Nanney says, "and all have subtle variation, the yarn is wonderful for a beginning knitter. You can do a simple project with a little trim and still have something interesting."

Her yarns and sweaters have become the foundation of Seacolors, a company Nanney named for the unique shades her dyeing methods produce. She herself learned to knit when she was five, taught by her grandmother, "probably to get me to sit down and be quiet," she jokes. "But I only knit for family and close friends."

For Seacolors, she creates the designs for the sweaters, many of which are variations on a single pattern: a square tunic with an opening to accommodate one's head. But what variations! The garments can be knit short, long, or asymmetrical and distinguished with a dizzying array of collars, sleeves, edgings, and handspun trim details. Some of the sweaters are closed, fittingly, with sea-glass or beach-stone buttons.

Nanney chooses the colors, styles, and finishes, and subcontracts the actual knitting to a few local women who work on knitting frames at home in rural Maine. She'll sell the sweaters, among other places, at the round of wool fairs and crafts markets that take place from Maine to Maryland and beyond, from summer till December.

Over time the shows have proved to be a fruitful source of ideas and feedback. They allowed her to "do a little market research, find out what styles people liked and their color preferences. Blue and green are always popular," she notes, "and now orange is selling really well."

Along with her yarns and sweaters, Nanney has been taking a new line of Maine blankets to the fairs—the product of another of her companies, called Get Wool. Soft,

Nanney hauls salt water (below) from the Damariscotta River; she uses it as she dyes yarn in her "downward dog" style (right).

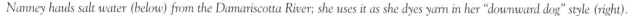

Out of the dye vat, skeins of yarn hang on the drying rack.

light, and creamy white, the throws are striped and edged with her delicately tinted yarns. The rest of the blankets' wool, however, comes not only from Nanney's sheep, but also from other wool growers in the state. "There are a lot of small flocks," she says, "with twenty or fewer sheep." To fill out the amount of fiber she requires, she'll go to specific farmers who have the potential to produce the kind of wool she wants and pay a premium for it.

A stately, almost-finished wooden barn dominates the space between Nanney's house and the dye vats. It's a long-term project that has occupied her for the last six years and is the focus of many of her future plans. "We'll have sheds on the side for lambing," she says with her characteristic verve, "and space for an office. The barn will have production rooms for knitting and designing, and there will be an apartment on top." The latter could be rented out to spinners and dyers who want to see what life on a fiber farm is like, to farm-stay guests curious about fiber on the hoof, or to Border Collie owners who want to train their dogs. "My secret hope is that anyone who comes will be able to learn to apply sustainable living to their own lives," she adds.

For now, though, the inside of the barn is nothing but bare studs surrounded by construction supplies. A white-pine and canvas canoe hangs from the rafters in front of the open rear doorway, which frames a gorgeous sunset view of the farm and the animals. The canoe is the last of fifty that once belonged to Nanney's grandfather, who was a celebrated outdoor guide in Baxter State Park in north-central Maine. On a fall day, the floor beneath the graceful craft is jammed with barrel-size burlap bags filled to overflowing with raw wool.

The fiber comes in a range of shades—white, gray, black, and a brown called moorit—all colors that evidence another of Nanney's passions. Both she and Ian Stewart have been supporters of the Black Sheep Society, which promotes naturally colored sheep raised for fiber. The group publishes a newsletter, to which Ian contributes articles, and holds periodic national gatherings.

Every five years there's an international congress, too, and the very idea throws Nanney's imagination into overdrive. The next one, in 2009, takes place in Brazil. "Why not take a trade mission of Maine wool farmers there?" Nanney suggests. "Then we can bring the next congress back here, to Maine," she says. "That's in 2014."

In the meantime, Nanney has plenty on her plate. There's the farm, Seacolors, and Get Wool to run, her sons to look after, dogs to train, and her barn to finish. She talks about what she does in the most expansive, inspiring terms: With her wool, her sweaters and blankets, her animals, and her dyes, she says, "I feel that I've stored all the summer and the energy, and the seawater and the colors, and the sustainability in the fibers themselves—and that's what people take home with them."

Ollie's Cardigan

Designer: Pat Roinestad

Nanney wears this as her all-around favorite, everyday sweater, so she named it for her favorite all-around herding dog, Ollie. The playful, mismatched vintage buttons and subtle cables lend it some of the exuberance that Ollie brings to his farm work.

Skill Level
Easy/Intermediate

Sizes
Women's Small (Medium, Large)

Finished Measurements
Chest: 40 (43½, 47)" (101.5 [110.5, 119.5]cm)
Length: 21 (22, 23)" (53.5 [56, 58.5]cm)

Materials
Seacolors, 100% wool, hand-dyed, worsted-weight yarn, 215 yd (196.5m), 4 oz (113.5g) per skein: 2 skeins in sky blue (color A); 2 skeins in plum (color B); 2 skeins in twilight gray (color C); and 1 skein in apricot-plum (color D)

US size 8 (5mm) needles, or size needed to obtain gauge
Cable needle
4 large buttons, at least 2" (5cm) in diameter

Gauge
14 stitches and 22 rows = 4" (10cm) in stockinette stitch

Special Abbreviations
Front Cable (fc): Knit to the 5 stitches to be cabled, put the next 3 stitches onto the cable needle, hold in front of the work, knit the next 2 stitches, then knit 3 stitches from the cable needle.
Back Cable (bc): Purl to the 5 stitches to be cabled, put the next 2 stitches onto the cable needle, hold in back of the work, purl the next 3 stitches, then purl 2 from the cable needle.

Pattern Stitches
The special cable stitches, front cable and back cable, are for texture. These are 3 x 2 cables knit over 5 stitches, *without* any set up stitches preceding or following, so they appear as ripples in the knitted fabric.

Back
Beginning at the hem with color C, cast on 58 (64, 70) stitches.
Rows 1–6: Work 6 rows in stockinette stitch, ending with a right side row facing.
Row 7 (fc): K5 (8, 10), *fc over the next 5 stitches, k6; repeat from * to last 9 (1, 11) stitches; **small size**, end fc, k4, **medium (large) sizes** end k1 (11).
Rows 8–13: Work 6 rows in stockinette stitch.
Row 14 (bc): P11 (2, 4), *bc over the next 5 stitches, p6; repeat from * to last 3 (7, 0) stitches; **small size**: p3; **medium size**: bc, p2.
Rows 15–20: Work 6 rows in stockinette stitch.
Row 21 (fc): Repeat row 7.
Rows 22–27: Work 6 rows in stockinette stitch, increase 1 stitch by working into the front and back of first and last stitches at each edge on row 24—60 (66, 72) stitches.

Change to color A and knit in stockinette stitch until work is 15 (16, 17)" (38 [40.5, 43]cm), or desired length, to neckline from the top of the cable hem. AT THE SAME TIME, increase 1 stitch by working into the front and back of the first and last stitches each side every 6 rows 5 times—70 (76, 82) stitches.

Shape Neck
With the right side facing, knit across 25 (28, 31) stitches. Join with a second skein of yarn and bind off the center 20 stitches, work to the end of the row. Working both sides at the same time with separate skeins of yarn, bind off 2 stitches at the neck edge at the beginning of every other row twice, work 2 rows straight—6 rows of neck shaping total. Bind off the remaining 21 (24, 27) stitches on each side for the shoulders.

Right Front
Note
Read this section through before working Right Front; pattern and buttonhole happen simultaneously. Only Right Front will have 2-stitch buttonholes on center Front, worked over the third and fourth stitches from the center edge. Place the first buttonhole on the fifth row. The second, third, and fourth buttonholes are approximately 4" (10cm) apart, depending on the size of the buttons you choose.

Beginning at the hem with color C, cast on 29 (32, 35) stitches. Knit 4 rows, ending with the right side facing for first cable row.

Row 7 (fc): K6 (8, 4), *fc over the next 5 stitches, k6; repeat from * to the last 1 (2, 9) stitches; **sizes small and medium**: k1 (2); **size large**: fc, k4.

Rows 8–13: Work 6 rows in stockinette stitch.

Row 14 (bc): P11 (2, 9), *bc over the next 5 stitches, p6; repeat from * to the last 7 (8, 4) stitches; **sizes small and medium**: bc, p2 (3); **size large**: p4.

Rows 15–20: Work 6 more rows in stockinette stitch.

Row 21 (fc): Repeat row 7.

Rows 22–27: Work 6 rows in stockinette stitch, increase 1 stitch by working into the front and back of the last stitch of the row at the side edge on row 24—30 (33, 36) stitches.

Change to color A and work, for 12 (13, 14)" (30.5 [33, 35.5]cm), or to desired length of neckline increasing by working into the front and back of the last stitch of the row on every sixth row 5 times—35 (38, 41) stitches.
AT THE SAME TIME, work buttonholes on the fifth row and every 4" (10cm) as follows:

Buttonhole Row 1: K2, bind off the next 2 stitches, work in pattern to the end of the row.

Buttonhole Row 2: Work in pattern, casting on 2 stitches over the stitches bound off on the previous row, p2.

Shape Neck

When work is your desired length to neckline, change to color D and, at the neck edge, bind off 6 stitches. Work to end of row. Now bind off 2 stitches on every other right-side row at neck edge 4 times, continue to work to the same length as the Back, bind off.

Left Front

Beginning at the hem with color C, cast on 29 (32, 35) stitches. Knit 4 rows, ending with the right side facing for first cable row.

Row 7 (fc): K1 (2, 4), *fc over the next 5 stitches, k6; repeat from * to the last 6 (8, 4) stitches; k 6 (8, 4).

Rows 8–13: Work 6 rows in stockinette stitch.

Row 14 (bc): P2 (3, 4), *bc over the next 5 stitches, p6; repeat from * to the last 11 (2, 9) stitches, p11 (2, 9).

Rows 15–20: Work 6 more rows in stockinette stitch.

Row 21 (fc): Repeat row 7.

Rows 22–27: Work 6 rows in stockinette stitch, increase 1 stitch by working into the front and back of the first stitch of the row (at the side edge) on row 24—30 (33, 36) stitches.

Change to color A and work for 12 (13, 14)" (30.5 [33, 35.5]cm), or to desired length of neckline, increasing at the beginning of the row (side edge using the method as before) on the sixth row 5 times—35 (38, 41) stitches.

Shape Neck

When work is your desired length to neckline (right-side facing), change to color D and knit 1 row. On the next row, at the neck edge, bind off 6 stitches. Work to the end of the row. Now bind off 2 stitches on every other wrong-side row at the neck edge 4 times, continue to work to the same length as the Back, bind off.

Sleeves

With color C, cast on 32 stitches.

Rows 1–6: Work in stockinette stitch for 6 rows, ending with the right side facing for the first cable row.

Row 7: Knit 4 stitches, *fc over the next 5 stitches, k5; repeat from * to the last 8 stitches, fc, k3.

Rows 8–13: Work 6 rows in stockinette stitch.

Row 14: K9, *fc, k5; repeat from * to the last 3 stitches, k3.

Rows 15–20: Work 6 rows in stockinette stitch.

Row 21 (fc): Repeat row 7.

Rows 22–27: Work 6 more rows in stockinette stitch.

Row 28: Change to color B, and work increase row, *k5, m1, k4, m1; repeat from * twice, ending k5—38 stitches. Continue in stockinette stitch and shape sides by increasing 1 stitch by working into the front and back of the first and last stitches at each edge every 4 rows 4 times, then every 6 rows 9 times—64 stitches. Continue knitting straight to 19" (48.5cm) or desired Sleeve length. Bind off all stitches.

Finishing

Sew shoulder seams. Measure down 9" (23cm) on each side from the shoulder for Sleeve placement. Set in and sew Sleeves. Sew side seams only to the top of color C to have the texture border open at the sides. Weave in all ends. Using a crochet hook, work crab stitch around hem, cuff, neckline, and Fronts with color of choice as follows: single crochet around the edge. Chain 1, do not turn, reverse single crochet around all stitches to the end. Trim yarn and weave in end.

Sew on 4 large buttons across from the buttonholes.

Border Collies, like Ollie, love cooling off after a bit of hard work.

Ollie's Cardigan

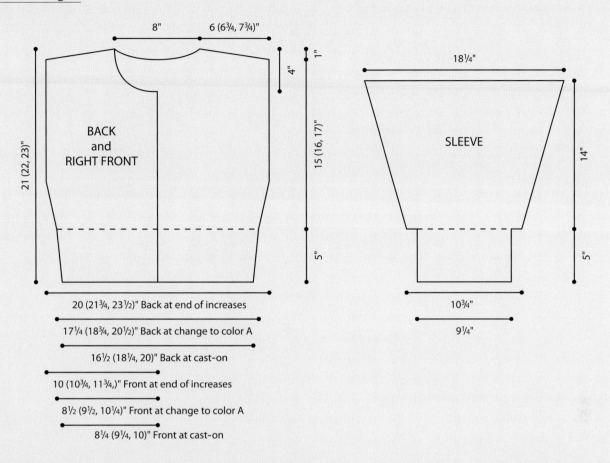

BACK
and
RIGHT FRONT

SLEEVE

8"

6 (6¾, 7¾)"

4"

1"

15 (16, 17)"

5"

21 (22, 23)"

18¼"

14"

5"

20 (21¾, 23½)" Back at end of increases

17¼ (18¾, 20½)" Back at change to color A

16½ (18¼, 20)" Back at cast-on

10 (10¾, 11¾,)" Front at end of increases

8½ (9½, 10¼)" Front at change to color A

8¼ (9¼, 10)" Front at cast-on

10¾"

9¼"

Low Tide Crossover Vee Sweater

Designer: Pat Roinestad

Although it looks like a cardigan, this faux-kimono-style sweater is stitched down and worn as a pullover. You can substitute any commercial or handspun laceweight yarn you wish for the trim. Nanney likes to use silk for a dressier finish or a natural handspun wool of varying thickness for an earthier look.

Skill Level
Intermediate

Sizes
Women's Small (Medium, Large)

Finished Measurements
Chest: 36½ (40, 43½)" (93.5 [101.5, 110.5]cm)
Length: 20 (21, 22)" (51 [53.5, 56]cm)

Materials

Meadowcroft Seacolors, 100% wool, hand-dyed, worsted-weight yarn, 215 yd (196.5m), 4 oz (113.5g) per skein: 3 skeins in steel blue (color A); 1 skein in rose quartz (color B); and 1 skein in gold (color C)

160 yd (146.5m) of handspun singles or any laceweight yarn for trim

US size 9 (5.5mm) needles, or size needed to obtain gauge
Stitch markers
US size F-5 (3.75mm) crochet hook for trim
Sea-glass buttons, any size, since they are decorative

Gauge
14 stitches and 22 rows = 4" (10cm) in stockinette stitch

Special Stitch
Cluster stitch: Working each double crochet stitch to the point where 2 loops remain on the hook, work 3 double crochet in next stitch, yarn over and draw through all loops on hook.

Back

With color A, cast on 64 (70, 76) stitches.
Knit in stockinette stitch for 6 (8, 8) rows, decrease 1 stitch by working 2 stitches together each side on row 7 (8, 8), then decrease each side every following fourth row 6 times—50 (56, 62) stitches. Work even until the piece measures 5½ (6, 6)" (14 [15, 15]cm) from the beginning.

Next row: Increase 1 stitch by working into the front and back of the first and last stitches of the row each side on the next row, then every fourth row 6 times—64 (70, 76) stitches. Work even until the piece measures 11 (12, 13)" (28 [30.5, 33]cm) from the beginning.

Shape Armhole
Bind off 2 stitches at the beginning of the next 2 rows—60 (66, 72) stitches. Decrease 1 stitch at each side edge every other row 3 times—54 (60, 66) stitches. Work even until the armhole measures 7½" (19cm).

Shoulder and Neck Shaping
At 18 (18½, 19)" (46 [47, 48.5]cm) from the beginning, knit across 17 (20, 23) stitches, then join the second ball of yarn and bind off the center 20 stitches. Working both sides at the same time, bind off 2 stitches at the neck edge every other row 3 times—6 stitches decreased on each side. Knit 2 rows in stockinette stitch, then bind off the remaining 11 (14, 17) stitches for each shoulder.

Left Front

With color B, cast on 46 (49, 52) stitches. Knit in stockinette stitch for 6 (8, 8) rows and begin the first decrease at the side edge (the beginning of the row), then every fourth row 6 times. Work even until the piece measures 5½ (6, 6)" (14 [15, 15]cm) from the beginning. Increase 1 stitch by working into the front and back of the first stitch on the side of the next row, then every following fourth row 6 times. AT THE SAME TIME, when the piece measures 5" (13cm) from the beginning, place a marker at the center Front and begin the decreases as follows: with the wrong side facing, decrease 1 stitch by working the first 2 stitches together at the neck edge on this row and every other row 22 (19, 16) times, then every following fourth row 8 (11, 14) times. AT THE SAME TIME, when work measures 11 (12, 13)" (28 [30.5, 33]cm) from the beginning, begin armhole shaping. Bind off 2 stitches at the beginning of the next row, then decrease 1 stitch at the beginning of the next 3 right-side rows. You should have the same number of stitches as for the Back shoulder—11 (14, 17) stitches. Continue to work to the same length as the Back, bind off.

Right Front

With color C, cast on 46 (49, 52) stitches. Knit in stockinette stitch for 6 (8, 8) rows and begin the first decrease at the side edge (the end of the row), then every fourth row 6 times. Work even until the piece measures 5½ (6, 6)" (14 [15, 15]cm) from the beginning. Increase 1 stitch by working into the front and back of the last stitch on the side edge of the next row, then every following fourth row 6 times. AT THE SAME TIME, when the piece measures 5" (13cm) from the beginning, place a marker at the center Front (the beginning of the row) and begin the decreases as follows: decrease 1 stitch by working the first 2 stitches of the row together at the neck edge on this row and every other row 22 (19, 16) times, then every following fourth row 8 (11, 14) times. AT THE SAME TIME, when work

measures 11 (12, 13)" (28 [30.5, 33]cm) from the beginning, and with the wrong side facing, begin armhole shaping. Bind off 2 stitches at the beginning of this next row, then decrease 1 stitch at the beginning of the next 3 wrong-side rows. You should have the same number of stitches as for the Back shoulder—11 (14, 17) stitches. Continue to work to the same length as the Back, bind off.

Sleeves

With color A, cast on 34 stitches. Work in stockinette stitch, increasing 1 stitch by knitting into the front and back of the first and last stitches on each side on the fifth and every following fourth row 13 (13, 14) times—60 (60, 62) stitches. Work even until the piece measures 14" (35.5cm) from the beginning.

Cap Shaping

Bind off 3 stitches at the beginning of the next 2 rows, then bind off 2 stitches at the beginning of the next 6 rows. Decrease 1 stitch by knitting the first (and last) 2 stitches together on each side every other row 8 times. Bind off remaining stitches.

Finishing

Sew both shoulder seams, set in Sleeves, and sew side seams. Weave in all ends. Work crochet trim with handspun as follows: with crochet hook, work 1 row single crochet around all edges; next row, single crochet in first stitch, *chain 3, cluster stitch in the next stitch, skip 2 stitches, single crochet in the next stitch; repeat from * around all edges. Fasten off.

When crochet trim is complete, lap right front over left, and then try the sweater on before tacking on the inside. Note that the Right Front should not extend completely to the left side seam. Sew on 2 buttons through both thicknesses. Place a third button higher up for better closure, sewing it closed.

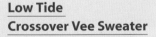

Low Tide
Crossover Vee Sweater

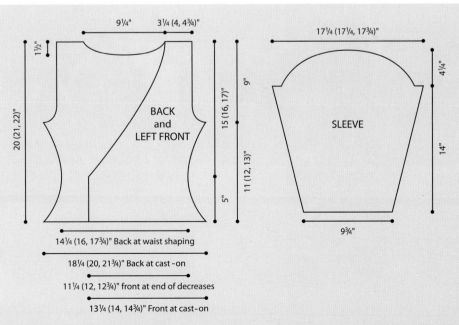

Tregellys Fiber Farm

A Global View
From Sheep to Yaks

Hawley, Massachusetts

Fiber on the hoof (opposite)—Tregellys's llamas, goats, and sheep. Above (clockwise from top left): Botanical Shades's dyed wool, Tibetan yak, cable detail with Botanical Shades yarn, sunflower in bloom.

ibetan prayer flags flutter at the entrance to Tregellys Fiber Farm, adding rainbow colors to the green, tree-shaded slopes of Hog Mountain and giving the first hint that this is not one of the usual dairy farms around Hawley, in western Massachusetts. The animals that populate the yards and paddocks provide even clearer evidence of Tregellys' distinctiveness. In addition to half a dozen rare or heritage breeds of sheep, there are Angora goats, Bactrian camels, llamas, alpacas, yaks, cows, yak-cow crosses called Dzos, a couple of donkeys, an assortment of dogs, chickens, turkeys, and swans, and one guard emu. And, oh yes, there is also a sixteen-foot-high Tibetan stone stupa.

The stupa, a kind of Buddhist shrine, is a relatively new addition, built about three years ago near the 1806 stone and cedar-shake farmhouse that is the heart of the property that Ed and Jody Cothey bought in the early 1990s and named Tregellys, which means "hidden homestead" in Cornish.

Tregellys today is a working farm with fiber animals, a weaving studio, and a natural dyeing business. But its story really begins an ocean away and a decade earlier in Cornwall, England, in 1982, with a chance encounter in an after-hours bar. Jody, then a thirty-six-year-old Massachusetts native, had won a Guggenheim fellowship to write poems inspired by Arthurian legends. Ed had just gotten off a fishing boat. Their five days' acquaintance was followed by an epistolary romance after Jody returned to the States. The next year she moved to England, and the couple were married.

Ed, who was born in 1953 in St. Ives, on England's southwest coast, had spent his life either on farms or at sea. His sailor's life is still visible in the form of tattoos that cover his arms. As far as his farming life, Ed says he's been shoveling manure since he could stand up. "Cornwall has England's first daffodils, first anemones, first broccoli—what we call cauliflower here," he notes proudly, "and new potatoes." But he also grew up helping to fashion and repair herring nets in the living room. "Every winter we made

father's gear." And when Ed left school and became a seaman himself, he often played with string, doing macramé as a hobby. "Young girls loved my belts, so I made a lot of belts," he recalls, and he sold a few things for "beer money."

The Cotheys spent seven years in England, with Ed adding photography to his other skills, before they moved to Massachusetts in 1990. Intrigued by the idea of raising llamas, the couple eventually bought 138 acres of woods on a north-facing slope in the foothills of the Berkshires. Known as the Dodge farm, the land came with a two-hundred-year-old clapboard Cape Cod that had been put back together by the previous owners but not restored. The original ax marks are still visible on the chestnut beams that support the ceiling.

It's a comfortable house, Jody notes, two stories with open space around a central chimney, a bay window in the back, and plywood walls now painted aqua and butternut. It took a few months to put in electricity and a phone; meanwhile, the Cotheys cleared fifty acres, which gave them a view of Vermont's Mount Snow in the distance. They traded a wood chipper for four dairy goats, acquired two pigs and two sheep, and started building barns.

In the fluid mix of entrepreneurial spirit, artistic vision, and sheer love of animals that characterizes Tregellys, however, Ed soon became enamored of Angora goats. Before long the dairy goats (which had proved difficult to milk) went elsewhere, and several llamas took their places in the barns. Over time, the couple added more sheep, a Baudet du Poitou donkey, Royal Pinto yaks, and Bactrian camels.

"All of this just sort of happened," remembers Jody, who adds that in the process "we realized we really did have to think about fiber." Because producing fiber was what many of these animals were about. If you have Angora goats, "all of a sudden you've got mohair."

An Angora goat (opposite) seems unflappable as wind riffles prayer flags on the stupa nearby. Above: the Cotheys' house.

The Cotheys embarked on a process of self-education. "We read; we had to learn about parasite care," she says. By the mid 1990s, Ed was having yarn processed from wool and mohair, and through participation in CISA (Community Involvement in Sustaining Agriculture), an umbrella organization that helps small farmers market their products, they met Jody McKenzie, a sheep farmer, weaver, and natural dyer. Over time, the number of Angora goats dwindled, and different breeds of rare and heritage sheep were brought on.

"Ed took a weaving class," says Jody Cothey. "I learned to spin." When they built a separate weaving studio, they made space for a dyeing business on the bottom floor and asked McKenzie to run it. Since 2004 she has owned that enterprise, called Botanical Shades.

⊙

The day begins early at Tregellys Fiber Farm, with a mixture of routine chores and unexpected events to deal with. Jody, who rises between four thirty and five in the morning, might steal a little time to read poetry before she showers

and comes down to the kitchen and the bay-window panorama—"a drop-dead-gorgeous view," in Ed's words. Immediately there are eight dogs to feed: a Newfoundland, two collie mixes, a Chihuahua, a Shetland sheepdog, a Jack Russell, and two unusual guard dogs (an Italian Maremma and a Turkish Akbash). Cat waste also has to be picked up. Jody is straightforward about the realities of rural life. "All our pastoral adoration of farms . . . you can't have a tidy farm," she says. "They're messy. There are piles of string and wires, and animals poop all the time."

She finds a moment for cereal, toast, and yogurt and begins her tasks, sometimes relying on part-time workers to help feed out the hay, make sure the animals' water is clean, or sweep out the barns and stalls.

Meanwhile Ed gets going around six or six thirty. "The worst thing for Jody is if I come down the stairs at the same time," he says. He makes his breakfast of cereal and fruit and takes the dogs for a walk in the woods.

The farm is dotted with thirteen ponds and a variety of stalls and enclosures. Tregellys' big, blue barn is connected by a sunny "Arizona room" to a green barn, which houses camels—geldings, mothers, and their sons. The bull camel

Ed Cothey at work in the weaving studio.

Jody Cothey (above) plies a dyed fiber strand. Farm animals include a yak and calf (center) and a Bactrian camel (right), being combed by Ed for its luxuriant down.

has his own space. The buck shed, named for its former goat inhabitants, is now home to the llamas and donkeys. And prefabricated, arched Quonset huts, enclosures for birds, and sheds abound. "Wal-Mart carports make really good buildings," Jody says, "but they're not beautiful."

The business of animal husbandry is not an easy fit with Jody's continuing work as a poet. "I try my very hardest to write," says Jody, who has published several books, "and don't do much of it." On Tuesday mornings she often meets a small group of writers at a local coffee shop. "There are four of us in the group. We sit and talk and write a little. It's hard, but I like what I've done in the last year."

On most days, however, Jody works on the farm. In the morning, she prepares minerals for the animals' food. "We have our own mixture," she says, "with salt—all animals need salt—kelp, sheep mineral mix, powdered garlic, and edible diatomaceous earth." Afternoons are filled with more chores. "We go to the dump and deal with paperwork. Because the farm gets outside visitors, the United States Department of Agriculture (USDA) has us write everything that happens to each animal."

The phone rings all the time, plus there are errands to run, things to clean, and e-mails to answer. And always there is fiber to deal with.

Twice a year, local shearer Andy Rice comes to shear the fleece from the sheep and goats. That leaves a lot of fiber to be sorted and cleaned. "If I sell it, I like to go over it really carefully," Jody says. "You have to get as much vegetative matter out as possible. Most of our sheep now

don't have super-soft fiber." It's less suitable for knitting yarn. But they produce spinning fiber, and "now there's a lot of interest in felting.

"We don't get any fiber from the donkeys," she adds, but the yaks have a soft down that has to be brushed out, as well as a long skirt of coarse fiber that may be sheared, spun, or woven.

"Llamas we shear ourselves in the summer," Jody says. "It's not very hard. And the camels we brush out over three weeks around late May or June. They're naked all summer." The soft, luxurious camel down may be sold to hand spinners for a luxury yarn. The guard hair goes to people who want it for rope or for tying flies.

When it comes to actually working with wool or down or mohair, Jody says she is "an upper-beginning fiber person. I will hand spin and play with felt, and I'll prepare it for other people," she says. "I might clean it for roving," for example, referring to the rope-like strips of fibers that can also be felted, woven, or knit. But she sees herself mostly as "earth mother and secretary. Ed is the fiber artist."

Indeed, most of Ed's day is spent at one or another of his six looms—the five in the free-standing weaving studio or the huge Dobby rug loom in an upstairs weaving room in the house. He took up the craft seven years ago, learning from Becky Ashenden at nearby Vav Stuga, which means "weaving studio" in Swedish.

"When Becky was in college, she fell in love with Swedish weaving," Ed says, and she followed that interest by studying Swedish and traveling to the Scandinavian country. "She learned, came back, and taught me."

For someone who had worked on fishermen's nets and macramé decades ago, weaving was a natural fit. "I'm

Ed's woven throws incorporate intricate designs.

severely dyslexic," he says; "I never read a book, and I don't look at weaving magazines. But if someone shows me something, I can replicate it. I see the pictures in my head."

Ed found he had the ability to visualize a finished piece before he threaded the loom, an exacting and time-consuming task that could take a week or a month, depending on the loom.

He starts by putting on the warp—the lengthwise threads—and has a pattern harness on each of those strands. On the biggest loom, which is twelve feet wide, compressed air helps lift the harnesses, but Ed uses a manual beater to compress them and rug shuttles to draw the horizontal weft threads from one end to the other.

"Sometimes I weave with five, six, or seven strands together in the weft," he says. "It's more artistic. It gives a lot more range of color and texture. I'll weave a four-inch plain border. Then I start playing with the pattern harnesses." He feels free to improvise. "In little blocks I can do any sort of pattern. I make it up. Well, some I draw in advance, but lately, with, say, a monastery scene, I make it as I go. I never do the same thing twice."

Ed works on half a dozen pieces at once. On any given day he might have a rug on the big loom and a twin-size blanket, a throw, a dog bed, another blanket, and multicolor shawls on the others.

If he's weaving shawls, he'll thread enough warp for seven or eight at a time, leaving twelve inches between them for knots and a fringe on each of the finished products. "I'm trying to use up our sheep wool," he says, "and I'd like to get some llama yarn made, and use some of our own mohair," which he's also mixed with camel. "It feels softer than some weaving." But typically he draws fiber from many sources: "I buy cotton, linen, and other wool; there's a great mill-end shop near us."

Straight weaving goes fairly quickly. "I can do an afghan with no pattern, seventy inches long and fifty inches wide, in a day. With a pattern it might take two, three, or even four days."

The results are striking works of art. "I don't do boring stuff," Ed emphasizes. "I don't see the point. Life is short."

In a spacious studio under Ed Cothey's weaving workshop, Jody McKenzie, the proprietor of Botanical Shades, is busy dyeing wool.

"I always was fascinated with things like fabric and fiber," says Jody, who grew up near Boston and moved to a dairy farm in western Massachusetts around 1981, when she

Jody McKenzie (below, in vest, with Jody Cothey) reviews dyed roving that will become Botanical Shades yarn (right). Center: a Tregellys llama.

Jody McKenzie and her creations in the dyeing studio.

was twenty-five. "I was enamored with sheep. I learned to knit, though I wasn't great at it. And I have a master's certificate in weaving. Weaving and dyeing . . . that's my focus."

Jody has her own small flock of Coopworth and Romney sheep, and a decade ago, when she, like the Cotheys, belonged to CISA, she noticed that although members of the group were selling yarn on the side, the fiber was only white, brown, and gray. There were no colors.

"I decided to teach them to dye with natural dyes," she said, and organized a workshop for the group. "It's a hands-on learning process, difficult to learn from a book."

When Ed asked her to consult on setting up a dyeing business at Tregellys, she readily agreed. "But doing something on a kitchen stove is different from doing it on a commercial basis in thirty- to sixty-gallon vats," she says. She brought in her own consultant, Earthhues entrepreneur Michele Wipplinger, and went on to set up, run, and eventually take over the farm's yarn-coloring business.

These days the yarns she dyes rarely come from Tregellys' animals. "I buy wool and mohair and try to get it from local farmers. Most of my yarns are for knitting; they're softer. They must be clean and a certain quality and length." And though she pays premium prices, sometimes she has trouble getting enough to fulfill her commissions.

The actual dyeing process usually extends over four days. Working with fifty pounds of yarn, or occasionally raw fiber, at a time, Jody starts by seeing that the skeins are tied properly. "Every skein is weighed by the gram," she says. "Everything has to be really accurate."

To ensure that the color adheres to the yarn—and matches one of the thirty hues on her color card—the fiber must be free of lanolin. She uses dye extracts from around the world, which not only allow her to replicate her colors but also give her access to a wider range of tints.

"Colors tend to go with the climate," she observes. "There are no tropical hues from Massachusetts." And none of the extracts contains heavy metals; they're safe both for the dyer and the environment.

The first half-day is taken up with washing the yarn at two hundred degrees Fahrenheit; then she uses alum as a mordant, a substance that allows dyes to adhere to the fiber, and lets the yarn set overnight. Day two is for rinsing and spinning the fiber dry. On day three, the yarn goes back into the vats, according to color. There's one vat for indigo, four for all other colors.

"I heat it slowly over two to three hours to two hundred degrees Fahrenheit," she says, "hold it there for an hour, and let it all set overnight. The next day I take the yarn out of the dye vat, extract the water, wash it with vegetable-based soap, and hang it to dry.

"It takes a long time—measuring, mixing, heating, manipulating. Every day is different."

Several days a week, Tregellys is open to visitors. People may come to watch Ed in the weaving room or just to explore the farm. Schoolchildren are welcome, but Jody emphasizes that "this is a working farm, not a petting zoo." The Cotheys always try to include their community; for example, Jody sends out a notice during lambing season.

She says that "Ed gives a first-rate tour." He makes sure the visitors get to see every kind of animal. And in keeping with the farm's global approach, the visit includes a subtle geography lesson. "I tell them what country the animals are indigenous to, what they're used for, how they might mean life and death to their owners," Ed says.

His stories touch on fascinating facts about their Karakul sheep. For example, he might tell visitors that these colorful animals, originally from central Asia, are sometimes called Persian fat-tailed sheep. They're the only desert animal, Ed notes, that has renderable fat; you can actually make kosher bacon from them!

Or he might talk about Nigel, the emu. "He protects the water birds," Ed says, referring to the farm's swans. "Last week we had a mink that wanted them. But emus are great guardian birds. They can run faster than a fox and kick like a mule."

He clearly has a soft spot for the yaks, which arrived at Tregellys around 1998. Ed had gone to buy goats from a friend, saw the yaks, and came home with a pair of them as well. He eagerly passes along yak lore. "In Tibet," he says, "nomads usually live and travel in groups of three families, and yaks are raised in part of the tent. Tibetans have an affinity with the animal. It's everything to them: meat, milk, transportation. Bones and horns become prayer ornaments. They use every part of the yak except the grass in its stomach."

Jody tends to talk more about the animals' personalities. "Nothing beats a couple of yaks fooling around," she says. And though camels have a reputation for being unruly, Bactrians—the two-humped variety—"are super social. Our guys are really nice."

She seems to reserve her greatest affection for their forty sheep—six breeds that include Soay, Shetland, Icelandic, Navajo-Churro, Karakul, and Jacob. The last three are

Jody Cothey cradles an Angora kid.

considered rare. To Jody they're all individuals. "One of the Karakul was nervous and baaed a lot," she says. "When she had her first baby, she was aggressively maternal. It will be interesting to see what happens the next time."

She says the Soay—a small type of sheep that goes back to pre-Roman times in the British Isles—reminds her of alpacas in personality: "It's a complete dingbat, more skittish and involved in survival." Jody has crossed Soay and Shetland sheep in an attempt to develop a fiber that can be pulled out. "You don't shear Soay," she says.

There are fascinating aspects of each variety. The Jacob are recognizable by their badger faces and multiple horns; the Navajo-Churro, descendants of Iberian sheep brought by the Spanish to the Southwest, were nearly eradicated but have begun to be revitalized in the last thirty years. For each of the breeds there is a male on the farm, "except for the two Icelandic girls," Jody says.

Perhaps in the future they'll be joined by other varieties. There are breeds from all over the world to choose from. "I'd like to have a California Red sheep," Jody says, "and a Gotland. . . . I'd love one of every kind of interesting sheep!"

The Tibetan Connection

If Tregellys seems to have moved in a global direction, the reason may have something to do with the yaks. Shortly after the Cotheys bought them around 1998 a local newspaper carried a picture of the animals.

"The next day a bunch of monks walked by," Ed remembers. "They were looking for the yaks." It turns out there are more Tibetans than one might think in western Massachusetts. "And we got to know them."

"The Tibetans have a zillion fiber skills," Jody adds. And several members of the community, notably a sister and brother named Dheyang and Thinley, have worked part time—or lived—on the farm. It was Dheyang's husband, Lobsang, a recent American citizen, who built the stupa there as a memorial after 9/11.

"When it was finished, we had a big dedication ceremony with an interfaith service, and we invited the public," says Jody, who considers herself not so much Buddhist as an exploring person. "A stupa represents the mind of the compassionate Buddha, but it's more than one thing. We walk around it and say prayers."

Over the last four years the Cotheys' ties to the Tibetans have deepened, extending to refugees in Nepal. Ed has started to travel there annually, staying six or eight weeks at a time, and this year Jody joined him. The couple now sponsors Tibetan children, paying tuition, taking care of medical bills, and buying clothes. They've helped with businesses and begun to import handicrafts. The Tregellys shop that offers Ed's weaving now has a place for Tibetan and Nepali goods as well.

"We sell silver jewelry with real stones, lucky charms, prayer wheels, and pashmina shawls," Ed says. "There are four ladies in Nepal who weave, making bed covers in cotton. The profits go back to Nepal."

Tibet meets Massachusetts at Tregellys Fiber Farm.

Berkshire Tote

Designer: Karin Steinbrueck

A fun project for beginners who want to move on from scarves or for a more experienced knitter who wants a simple project to play with. Once you've made one tote, you can improvise by adding more colors or graphics on the sides. If you want to make a tote and hat set, three skeins of the Artisan Hemp Blend yarn is enough for both projects if you reverse the main and contrast colors.

Skill Level
Easy

Size
One size

Finished Measurements
Approximately 7" x 10" (18cm x 25.5cm) without strap

Materials
Botanical Shades Artisan Hemp Blend yarn, 27½% hemp, 27½% mohair, 45% wool, 290 yd (265m), 8 oz (227g) per skein: 1 skein in mulberry, main color (MC), and 1 skein in sage, contrast color (CC)

US size 6 (4mm) needles, or size needed to obtain gauge
Tapestry needle

Gauge
18 stitches and 24 rows = 5" (12.5cm) in stockinette stitch

Note
The tote is knit from the top down. Slipping stitches purlwise creates the "folds" that form the tote's shape.

Tote Body
With MC, cast on 69 stitches.
Row 1: K1, sl1p, k6, sl1p, k26, sl1p, k6, sl1p, k26.
Row 2: Purl.
Repeat rows 1 and 2 for 3" (7.5cm).
Work stripe pattern from chart (page 36), working stripes using the intarsia technique. When chart is finished, repeat rows 1 and 2 until piece measures 10" (25.5cm), ending with a right-side row.

Next row (WS): You are now working the bottom of the tote. Bind off 32 stitches, k28 (will show a purl on the right side), purl the remaining stitches.
Turn, bind off 7 stitches, work to the end.
Continue in stockinette stitch for 2" (5cm). Bind off the remaining stitches.

Tote Strap
With MC, cast on 14 stitches.
Row 1: K3, sl1p, k6, sl1p, k3.
Row 2: Purl.
Repeat rows 1 and 2 until the strap measures 30" (76cm) or the desired length. Bind off.

Fold the strap together lengthwise with right sides out.

Using MC, sew the strap together using mattress sewing stitch or another invisible sewing stitch.

Finishing
Working inside out, sew the bottom of the tote to the three sides. Sew the side seam. With the same or contrasting color, and working right-side out, sew the strap to the outside of the tote, about 2" (5cm) down from the top.

Weave in all the loose ends.

Angora kids and goats at play.

Berkshire Tote Chart Key

☐ Using MC, knit on RS, purl on WS.

◇ Using CC, knit on RS, purl on WS.

Ⅴ Slip 1 stitch purlwise.

☐ Stripe pattern is worked on Front only.

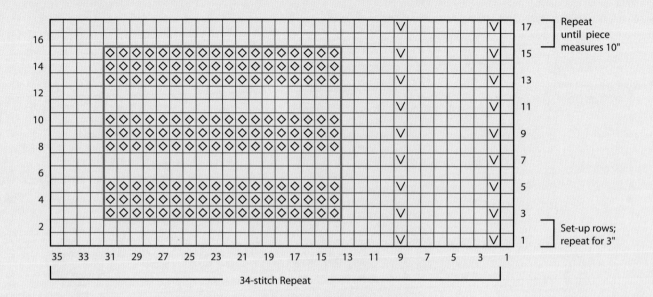

Repeat until piece measures 10"

Set-up rows; repeat for 3"

34-stitch Repeat

Festive looking fowl.

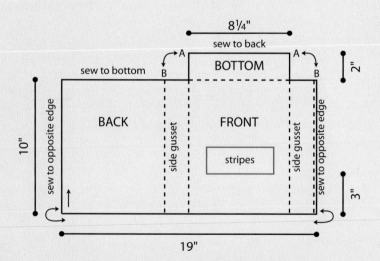

8¼"
sew to back
2"
sew to bottom
A → B — BOTTOM — A ← B
sew to opposite edge
10"
BACK   side gusset   FRONT   side gusset   sew to opposite edge
stripes
3"
19"

Fold point A to point B on both side gussets, sew seam.
Sew bound-off edge of Bottom to Back.
Sew side seam.

The Noho Boho Hat

Designer: Karin Steinbrueck

Named after the nearby eclectic town of Northampton, Massachusetts, this pattern is an artsy alternative to the good old wool beanie. The pillbox shape lets you play with combining colors. If you want your ears covered, add another round of purl and four more rounds of knit before you start to shape the crown.

Skill Level
Easy

Size
Adult

Finished Measurements
Circumference: 21" (53.5cm)

Materials
 Botanical Shades Artisan Hemp Blend yarn, 27½% hemp, 27½% mohair, 45% wool, 290 yd (265m), 8 oz (227g) per skein: 1 skein in sage, main color (MC), and 1 skein in mulberry, contrast color (CC)

US size 6 (4mm), 16" (40.5cm) long circular needle, or size needed to obtain gauge
US size 6 (4mm) set of 4 double-pointed needles
Stitch marker
Tapestry needle

Gauge
18 stitches and 24 rows = 5" (12.5cm) in stockinette stitch

Hat
With circular needle and CC, cast on 75 stitches.

Round 1: Knit 75 stitches. Join, taking care not to twist stitches and placing a marker to mark the beginning of the round.

Rounds 2–8: Work in stockinette stitch (knit every round). You have just completed the rolled edge in CC.

Fasten off CC. Join MC.

Purl Ridge: Purl 1 round.

Knit 6 rounds in stockinette stitch.

Purl Ridge: Purl 1 round.

Knit 5 rounds.

Purl Ridge: Purl 1 round.

Knit 5 rounds.

Purl Ridge: Purl 1 round.

Knit 5 rounds.

Note
You have worked a total of 24 rounds in MC.

Fasten off MC. Join CC.

Purl 1 round.

Knit 1 round.

Purl 1 round.

Knit 1 round.

Fasten off CC. Join MC.

Purl 1 round.

Shape Crown/Top of Hat
Change to double-pointed needles when the hat becomes too small for the circular needle.

Round 1: *K13, k2tog; repeat from * around—70 stitches.

Round 2: *K8, k2tog; repeat from * around—63 stitches.

Round 3: *K7, k2tog; repeat from * around—56 stitches.

Round 4: *K6, k2tog; repeat from * around—49 stitches.

Round 5: *K5, k2tog; repeat from * around—35 stitches.

Round 6: *K4, k2tog; repeat from * around—28 stitches.

Finishing
Break yarn, leaving about 4" (10cm) tail. Using the tapestry needle, thread yarn through the remaining stitches, pull tightly. Weave in all the loose ends.

Autumn House Farm

The Value of
Teamwork

Rochester Mills, Pennsylvania

The colors of October (opposite) at Autumn House Farm. Above (clockwise from top left): distinctive sheep markings, sign on the spinnery, hand-blended roving, hand-painted Finnean's Rainbow yarn.

nside an old summer kitchen at Autumn House Farm, in western Pennsylvania, Harriet Knox has accumulated a collection of household items—including washboards, irons, and canning kettles—that symbolize a century of "women's work" from around 1840 to 1940. Someday, she says, she'd like to arrange these objects into a formal display and possibly even organize a workshop on the topic.

The project doesn't seem all that far a stretch from the farmstead and craft workshops that already take place here, along with raising sheep and producing wool and yarn. And it certainly fits with Harriet's interest in the past and her support of traditional women's crafts. All that's lacking, perhaps, is the time.

Even time is probably not much of an obstacle, given Harriet's record of hard work and determination. Harriet's husband, Kenny Knox, points out that his wife has been president of a sheep and woolgrowers' association and has promoted the industry all over Pennsylvania. "If you could hold a snake," he says, with a mixture of pride and wry humor that comes with forty years of marriage, "Harriet would convince it to buy wool."

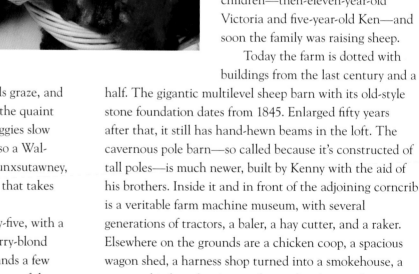

The Knoxes are taking a break on an autumn day to chat with a visitor who's come to see the farm, which sits at the top of Chestnut Ridge. Oak and maple trees crown the hills above the pastures where their animals graze, and the surrounding countryside suggests a mix of the quaint and the contemporary. Amish horse-drawn buggies slow traffic on the bucolic back roads, but there's also a Wal-Mart shopping center just five miles away in Punxsutawney, home to a famous Groundhog Day celebration that takes place every February.

Kenny is a big, barrel-chested man of sixty-five, with a green John Deere cap atop his graying strawberry-blond hair. He keeps his hands in his pockets and stands a few feet away from his wife, who is sitting on the steps of the carding house, where the fleece of their one hundred sheep is turned into artfully shaded roving. "She makes me crazy," he adds with apparent affection.

For her part, Harriet is quick to credit Kenny for the farm's success. Five years younger than her husband, she's a compact woman with a heart-shaped face framed by brown bangs and medium-length hair. Behind her glasses are penetrating hazel eyes that seem to add intensity to all her comments. "The relationship between a husband and wife is so important," she says. Aside from the need for mutual understanding, "farm life is physically demanding. And it calls for mental discipline."

But then discipline is no stranger to either of them. Harriet, who is third-generation military, grew up on stories of her mother's Welsh forbears who endured hard times on Florida ranches in the twenties and thirties. Kenny's Knox ancestors came here from Scotland in 1840 and worked the neighboring farm for three generations. The youngest of thirteen siblings, Kenny was driving wagons when he was four years old and went on to have a career in the Air Force. In 1970 he and Harriet bought this land, roughly a hundred acres, from an old family friend who maintained it for them while they were away. Almost a decade later, as Kenny finished his second tour of duty in Germany, Harriet returned with their children—then-eleven-year-old Victoria and five-year-old Ken—and soon the family was raising sheep.

Today the farm is dotted with buildings from the last century and a half. The gigantic multilevel sheep barn with its old-style stone foundation dates from 1845. Enlarged fifty years after that, it still has hand-hewn beams in the loft. The cavernous pole barn—so called because it's constructed of tall poles—is much newer, built by Kenny with the aid of his brothers. Inside it and in front of the adjoining corncrib is a veritable farm machine museum, with several generations of tractors, a baler, a hay cutter, and a raker. Elsewhere on the grounds are a chicken coop, a spacious wagon shed, a harness shop turned into a smokehouse, a summer kitchen that is now the carding house, the toolshed, and the Knox home.

At home in the barnyard (opposite). Above: Harriet Knox and hand-dyed locks in the carding house.

Constructed in 1894, their two-story farmhouse is furnished with family settees and sideboards, as well as photographs, boxes of yarn, cones of wool, and yes, a spinning wheel across from the fireplace. Correspondence and more yarn crowd the cloth-covered table in the dining room, where teal paint brightens a beadboard wall. In the kitchen, there's an imposing old ten-burner stove, and the family's two Border Collies, Whip and Jess, roam in and out.

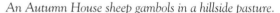

The morning sun illuminates the ewes grazing on the hillside, in one of the twenty-acre paddocks that extend like wedges from the farm buildings at the center. On this particular day the males of the flock are penned in the lower level of the barn. One of the Border Collies eyes the rambunctious animals into a corner, while Harriet tends to an aging ram.

The sheep here are bred to meet the farm's specific needs, she says. Karakul rams are crossed with Border Leicester ewes to achieve the desired tone and luster of fleece. The resulting "Karashires" are silver-gray in color with moorit (brown) and cinnamon highlights. The farm has also developed sheep with a spotted fleece and a badger face, as well as a newer mix with crimped lustrous wool and impressively curled horns, called Moorland Horns.

"The breeding, the idea that we can create what we need, has been so much fun," says Harriet. "We want the whole package—excellent conformation, meat, and fleece."

Producing the whole package calls for long days that begin between five thirty and six o'clock in the morning. "We grab a cup of coffee and sit on the porch and plan our day," Harriet says. "We might talk about something that happened the day before."

As their day gets going, Harriet often bakes biscuits. Kenny usually goes down to the basement and writes in his journal about the weather, the crops, or the animals.

"That's his private space." Harriet explains. "He figures out what he has to do outside—fieldwork or dealing with equipment." Harriet will eventually go upstairs and do office work or read animal husbandry magazines. Around seven o'clock they both go out and feed the animals.

They put down hay for any confined sheep, using oat straw, which generates heat—useful in winter—as it becomes compacted and solid. "We lime and straw a couple times a week," she says. The sheds are cleaned thoroughly twice a year. "We use the compost to fertilize the field. There are no pesticides in the barn," she notes, "and almost no flies. We rely on Muscovy ducks and barn swallows."

In the course of a day, the farm work is interspersed with wool work, such as carding, dyeing, spinning, or packing yarn. Lunch is almost nonexistent.

An Autumn House sheep gambols in a hillside pasture.

Kenny Knox (above) hefts a newborn lamb, while Harriet (right) has a double handful of twins. Center: Working on the haying machine.

"In winter I try to make myself quit around four or four thirty," Harriet says. "In the summer we work till dark. The evening feeding is around seven thirty, but there are only a few animals inside in warm weather." When Kenny and Harriet come out of the barn, they're usually holding hands "unless," Harriet adds, "we are having a 'discussion.'"

"I cook dinner, with salad and vegetables. We eat meat—usually lamb—almost every night. I might make it up till nine," she says. "But days don't turn out the way you plan. It's roll with the punches."

The daily routines, of course, are also geared to the rhythms of the year. "Our lives are regulated by the seasons," Harriet acknowledges. They breed the ewes in October and shear out their belly fleece around Thanksgiving. "As soon as we know that it will snow to stay, we shut the sheep in the barn." Lambing takes place in early March, and the rest of the flock is shorn in late April or early May.

When spring is near, "we can smell it," Harriet says. Kenny and the other farmers seem to react to something in the air. "You can see the men . . . feel their engines revving. June consists mostly of haying. Harvesting is August. By November everything is picked. Then, in late fall, we have a celebration on our shearing day."

To sustain the sheep in winter, Kenny leases additional fields and grows corn, oats, and hay, sometimes working with other farmers who, like him, grew up in these hills. He makes his own feed, mixing the grains with minerals, soy, distillers, and magnesium.

In fact, there's an overall emphasis on self-sufficiency and a philosophy of pay as you go. "We have gravity-fed water from five springs," Harriet says, "three to the barn and two to the house." Natural gas from wells on the farm provides fuel. Harriet and Kenny raise their own meat and get eggs

from their chickens. They buy their vegetables from friends who live nearby.

The farm relies heavily on Kenny's construction skills and mechanical abilities, which range from building barns and additions to keeping the aging tractors running and customizing the carding machines Harriet uses to process her wool. It's Kenny's innovative technical vision, his wife insists, that makes the production and manufacturing side of the farm as efficient and cost effective as it is. "It has made our business a viable reality," she says, adding, "We do all our own vet work, too. Kenny and I have to work as a team."

The combination of her art and Kenny's talents are integral to the economic success of Autumn House. "There are no more than ten of us in Pennsylvania with flocks of this size," she says. "You have to have modest expectations. And our fiber and art is value added," she explains. "It lets me stay on the farm, so I don't have to work elsewhere." And even though farm life is hard, that seems to pale in the face of what the family has accomplished.

The yarns that Autumn House produces are marvels of texture and color, both natural shades and dyed or blended in imaginative combinations. So it's not surprising to find out that Harriet's talents include several of the fine arts.

"I was a painter first," she says, but her family discouraged that as a career. After she and Kenny married in 1965, and he was stationed around the United States and abroad, she found ways to use and enlarge her talents. She ran a painting and pottery gallery in South Carolina, did needlework in Utah, and trained with a potter in Germany. "I had the privilege of working at the second-oldest salt pottery in Europe," she says. "I loved the painting; I loved the pottery. But in the end it was the color. . . . I love the in-depth complex color" of the dye work and the spinnery.

As for Harriet's interest in knitting, both her mother and grandmother were great knitters, she says, but it was really the experience of living in Germany in the mid-1970s that shaped her interest. "I learned to knit from the German ladies who did *haus stricken arbeit*—home knitting. A truck would come through with yarn and the pattern of the month, and all the ladies who could knitted like demons till it came around again. They received two marks (about fifty cents) apiece for their hats, mittens, and caps, yet the money was theirs, and you never saw them without their knitting needles."

When she and Kenny returned to the States, Harriet says she looked for the great, basic, tweeded wool yarns she remembered from Europe. What she found instead was acrylic polyester worsted. "So here on the farm I thought, I have my own sheep, I'll spin my own yarn!" And for more than twenty-five years, that's what she's been doing, along with a few other things.

"Our products are yarns and fleeces in all stages," says Harriet. When the sheep are sheared, the farm's fleeces are sorted, graded, and ready for scouring. "Kenny does all the scouring, using natural soaps, and he does the bulk yarn dyeing," she says. Occasionally the farm buys wool from other growers, "if we need a certain kind," she explains.

For help with designs and color, Harriet often works with her daughter, who lives on a farmstead a few miles away with her husband and two children. A photographer and graphic designer, Vicky is an integral part of the Autumn House business; son Ken has followed his father's path, joining the Air Force.

"We dye all the time," says Harriet. "We know when we start a color profile, we have to do a hundred skeins." The majority of the dye is used up in the process, she points out. After all, the land is theirs, and she's extremely protective of what goes into the wastewater. She's also very protective of her methods and dye formulas. The process takes place in the main house basement, but the operation is strictly off-limits to visitors.

Harriet is perfectly willing to show off the carding house, however, a small cottagelike building where great bags of wool crowd the floor. She demonstrates how the clean, dry wool is first put through a picker, which opens the fleece till it looks like cotton candy. The result is then fed through the carder, a primitive-looking contraption with pins that pull the fleece around a substantial bobbin, then spit it out as ropelike roving, ready to be hand spun.

What's most fascinating, though, is the magically artful way Harriet feeds the fleece into the carder. Over fluffs of heather-colored wool, for example, she might lay strands of dyed silk, linen, rayon, or Tencel threads, in color combinations she has worked out over the years. The roving that emerges might be any of a hundred colorways. Barleycorn, for example, is a rich brownish-gray with bits of grain-colored and terra-cotta silk and linen mixed in.

Autumn House uses two small mills for its basic spinning, then dyes the resulting yarns in its signature colors. But the farm's handspun and plied designer yarns are created by Harriet, Vicky, and several other women who work with them in an artists' cooperative that includes a spirit of collaboration reminiscent of the quilting bees and sewing circles that sustained women's crafts over the centuries. Eileen Fontana spins, felts, knits, and teaches others to knit. Delores Douglass, Sheri Franz, and Hanna Peck are adept at designing patterns. Kate Dinsmore is a weaver and a full-time partner in the dyeing and spinning. The group often gathers in the spinnery, a combination shop and studio that is connected to the farmhouse through a sunroom that Kenny built. There the walls are lined with brilliantly hued skeins of wool and silk and rayon yarns.

Hand-dyed fleece (below) on the carding house porch. Right: Sheri Franz (in red) and Hanna Peck feed locks into the carding machine.

Hanna, Sheri, and Harriet find a moment at harvest time to sit and spin.

Sweaters and other garments created by the fiber artists are also on display as examples of the farm's yarns and patterns. "A lot of our yarns are geared to outerwear," says Harriet, but she also points out a popular stocking design that they developed because "our customers wanted to get a sock done before the Second Coming!"

A dozen or so times a year, the Autumn House crew attend wool and craft shows, such as those in Glenwood, Maryland; Allegan, Michigan; or Rhinebeck, New York. "We work for three months to represent ourselves at a show," Harriet says, adding that Kenny usually drives her and other members of the cooperative who come to work the booth and meet the fiber enthusiasts who seek them out "because they want something different. If we're lucky, we have examples of each yarn profile: the diameter, the texture, the look."

Each fair has a slightly different character and kind of clientele, she notes: "In Maryland, they want estate clothing and a country look, and sometimes art clothing that's not 'Woodstock'—interesting complex garments. In Michigan, where they come out of the womb knitting, they like the 'Orbis' look—gray and white and art elements."

If the shows are a form of fiber "outreach," so, too, are the craft workshops that happen at Autumn House Farm

perhaps thirty weekends a year. Visitors can stay across the road in the cream-colored clapboard "dowry house" that Harriet and Kenny restored and dubbed "Shepherd's Rest." Built in 1870, the three-bedroom home still has heart-of-pine floors and antique furniture, like the five-board table that seats fourteen and a cherry cabinet from 1850. Kenny and friends have added a modern kitchen and baths. In the sitting room, a library of craft books fills a wall of shelves.

Harriet and Kenny tailor the workshops to what the participants want to learn and what they already know. The participants could be a few weavers or a knitting circle or a group of friends eager to learn more about fiber crafts and perhaps do a little antique hunting at the same time.

Sometimes couples curious about life on a modern farm, or who are thinking about buying one, will participate in a small farmstead workshop. They spend a week working as livestock stewards, learning the shepherd's skills of the season, exploring management and marketing practices.

"But if you're not born to this life," Harriet insists, "everyone in the family should sit down at the table and talk about it" before committing to the decision. The stresses can take their toll, unless everyone is prepared.

For Harriet and Kenny, it seems, the discussions and the decision were settled long ago. And they savor the rewards. "We're extremely proud to be still in the business after all the ups and downs in the past thirty years. And if we sold the land," she asks, "what would we do?"

Welsh Traveling Socks

Designer: Sheri Franz

While vacationing in Wales, designer Sheri Franz noticed a fellow tourist in the bus seat in front of her knitting a sock with an interesting texture. She asked the woman if she could take a closer look. The woman let her hold the sock, and she charted it out then and there. Sheri created this pattern after she came home to Pennsylvania.

Skill Level
Intermediate

Size
Women's Medium (US size 7–8)

Finished Measurements
Leg length: 6½" (16.5cm) (to top of heel)
Foot length: 9" (23cm)
Circumference at ball of foot: 8" (20.5cm)

Materials
1 skein Autumn House Farm Strideaway Shetland, 100% superwash wool, hand-painted, mill spun fingering-weight yarn, 450 yd (411.5m), 4 oz (113.5g), in Skye Sea Garden

US size 1 (2.25mm) set of 4 double-pointed needles, or size needed to obtain gauge
Stitch markers
Tapestry needle

Gauge
32 stitches = 4" (10cm) in pattern stitch

Pattern Stitch (multiple of 8 stitches)

Row 1: *K5, p3; repeat from * to the end of the round.
Row 2: *With yarn in front, slip 5 stitches (as if to purl), k3; repeat from * to the end of the round.
Row 3: *K5, p3; repeat from * to the end of the round.
Row 4: *K2, pick up yarn in front of the slip stitches and knit with the third stitch, k5; repeat from * to the end of the round.
Repeat rows 1–4 for pattern.

Socks

Cast on 64 stitches.
Divide onto 3 double-pointed needles as follows—needles 1 and 3, 21 stitches each; needle 2, 22 stitches. Join the stitches to work in the round, making sure they are not twisted. With needle 4, knit approximately 1" (2.5cm) of k2, p2 ribbing. Place a marker at the beginning of needle 1 and begin pattern stitch. Work until the cuff is 6½" (16.5cm), or desired length.

Heel Flap

Slip 32 stitches onto needle 1 to work the instep later.
On the remaining 32 stitches, work as follows:
Row 1: K1-tbl, k2, *slip purlwise with thread in back, k1; repeat from * to last 3 stitches, k2, slip last stitch purlwise with yarn in front.
Row 2: K1-tbl, k2, purl across to last 3 stitches, k2, slip last stitch purlwise with yarn in front.

Repeat these 2 rows 15 more times until there are 32 heel rows completed.

Turn the Heel

Knit 17 stitches, k2tog, k1, turn.
Row 1: Slip 1, p3, p2tog, p1, turn.
Row 2: Slip 1, knit until 1 stitch before gap, k2tog, k1, turn.
Row 3: Slip 1, purl to 1 stitch before gap, p2tog, p1, turn.
Repeat rows 2 and 3 until all stitches of heel flap are worked, ending with a knit row.

Divide these stitches onto 2 needles. With needle 4, pick up and knit 16 stitches along the side of the heel. Continuing the pattern from where you left off before turning the heel, work the 32 stitches on the instep needles. Pick up 16 stitches along the other side of the heel, and with the same needle, knit the stitches on the holding needle). All stitches are now on 3 needles with the beginning of the round at the middle of the heel.

Round 1: Needle 1, knit with needle 4 to 2 stitches before the end of needle, k2tog; needle 2, work pattern stitch across instep; needle 3, ssk, knit to end.
Round 2: Knit 1 round, working in pattern stitch across instep on needle 2.

On the veranda of Shepherd's Rest (left to right): Delores Douglass, Kate Dinsmore, felter Sandy Trimble, and Hanna Peck.

Repeat these 2 rounds until you have 64 stitches. Then divide the stitches evenly onto 3 needles and continue with pattern stitch across the 32 stitches of the instep and stockinette across the bottom of the sock until the sock foot is 7½" (19cm) long.

Shape Toe
(Work in stockinette stitch from this point on.)
Next round: *K2tog, k6; repeat from * around—56 stitches. Work 4 rounds even.
Next round: *K2tog, k5; repeat from * around—48 stitches. Work 3 rounds even.
Next round: *K2tog, k4; repeat from * around—40 stitches. Work 2 rounds even.
Next round: *K2tog, k3; repeat from *around—32 stitches. Work 1 round even.
Next round: *K2tog, k2; repeat from * around—24 stitches. Work 1 round even.
Next round: *K2tog, k1; repeat from * around—16 stitches. Work 1 round even.
Next round: *K2tog; repeat from * around—8 stitches.

Finishing

Cut the yarn, leaving an 8–10" (20.5–25.5cm) tail. Using a tapestry needle, draw up the remaining stitches, and weave the tail in securely.

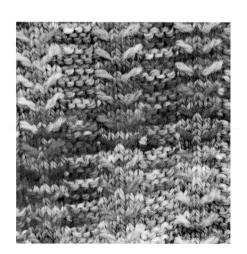

Cassandra Cardigan

Designer: Sheri Franz

An update on the classic cardigan, this elegant sweater is slightly cropped. It shows off the handspun luster of the first shearing of Autumn House Farm lambs. You can substitute another DK-weight yarn, but Harriet Knox encourages knitting the garment in handspun yarn and making it an "estate" project—a family heirloom that can be passed down from generation to generation.

Skill Level
Intermediate

Sizes
Women's Small (Medium, Large)

Finished Measurements
Chest: 39 (43, 47)" (99 [109, 119.5]cm)
Length: 22 (23, 24)" (56 [58.5, 61]cm)

Materials

10 (10, 12) skeins Autumn House Karashire, 100% wool, handspun, DK-weight yarn, 150 yd (137m), 3 oz (85g) per skein, for a total of 1,375 (1,500, 1,700) yd (1,257.5 [1,371.5, 1,554.5]m), in silver gray (Harriet sells the yarn for this project in "sweater lots" that are prepackaged according to the size of the sweater)

US size 4 (3.5mm) needles, or size needed to obtain gauge
US size 5 (3.75mm) needles
Cable needle
US size 4 (3.5mm), 29" (73.5cm) long circular needle
8 buttons, ½" (13mm) in diameter

Gauge
22 stitches and 30 rows = 4" (10cm) in stockinette stitch using size 4 (3.5mm) needles

Special Abbreviations
C4F (4-stitch cable): Slip 2 stitches onto cable needle, hold to the front of the work, k2, k2 from the cable needle.

Pattern Stitches

Cables and Ladders Pattern A
Row 1 (RS): K1, *p1, k4; repeat from *, ending k1.
Row 2 (WS): P1, *p1, k2, p1, k1, p4, k1; repeat from *, ending p1.
Row 3 (RS): K1, *p1, C4F, p1, k4; repeat from *, ending k1.
Rows 4 and 6 (WS): Work as for row 2.
Row 5 (RS): Work as for row 1.

Cables and Ladders Pattern B
Row 1 (RS): K1, *p1, k4; repeat from *, ending k1.
Row 2 (WS): P1, *p4, k1, p1, k2, p1, k1; repeat from *, ending p1.
Row 3 (RS): K1, *p1, k4, p1, C4F; repeat from *, ending k1.
Rows 4 and 6 (WS): Work as for row 2.
Row 5 (RS): Work as for row 1.

Back

Using larger needles, cast on 112 (122, 132) stitches. Knit 6 rows of garter stitch (3 garter ridges). Begin cables and ladders pattern A. Work in pattern until the piece measures 6½" (16.5cm), or desired length for cables and ladders border, ending with row 4 of pattern. Work another 4 rows in garter stitch (2 garter ridges), decreasing 6 (6, 4) stitches evenly across last row.

Decrease row: K15 (15, 24), k2tog, *k14 (16, 25), k2tog; repeat from * to the last 15 (15, 25) stitches, knit to the end— 106 (116, 128) stitches. Change to size 4 needles and continue in stockinette stitch until the Back measures 12½ (13, 13½)" (32 [33, 34.5]cm), ending with a wrong-side row.

Shape Armholes

Bind off 9 (10, 11) stitches at the beginning of the next 2 rows—88 (96, 106) stitches.

Decrease row: K1, k2tog, knit to the last three stitches, ssk.

Next row: Knit.

Repeat these 2 rows 8 (9, 11) times—72 (78, 84) stitches. Continue even until the piece measures 21 (22, 23)" (53.5 [56, 58.5]cm) from the beginning, ending with a wrong-side row.

Shape Shoulders and Back

Bind off 7 (7, 8) stitches at the beginning of the next 2 rows.

Left Shoulder

Bind off 6 (7, 7) stitches, work 3 (4, 4) stitches, work the next 2 stitches together, turn. Work 1 row even. Bind off the remaining stitches.

Back Neck and Right Shoulder

With right sides facing, rejoin the yarn to the remaining stitches, bind off the first 34 (36, 40) stitches, work to the end of the row. Bind off 6 (7, 7) stitches purlwise at the beginning of the next (wrong-side) row, p3 (4, 4) stitches, p2tog. Turn, knit 1 more row, bind off all stitches purlwise.

Left Front

With larger needles, cast on 57 (62, 67) stitches. Knit 6 rows in garter stitch (3 garter ridges). Change to cables and ladders pattern, repeat chart B across stitches for **small and large sizes**, repeat chart A for **medium size**.

Work cables and ladders pattern until front measures 6½" (16.5cm) or your desired length for the border, ending with row 4 of the pattern. Knit another 4 rows in garter stitch (2 garter ridges), decreasing 4 (3, 3) stitches evenly across last row as follows:

Decrease row: K11 (14, 16), k2tog, *k9 (14, 15), k2tog; repeat from * to the last 11 (14, 15) stitches, knit to the end—53 (59, 64) stitches.

Change to size 4 needles and continue in stockinette stitch until the Front measures the same as the Back to the armhole shaping, ending with a wrong-side row.

Shape Armholes and Neck

Bind off 9 (10, 11) stitches at the beginning of the next row. Now begin neck shaping at the beginning of the next (wrong-side) row, decrease 1 stitch by working p1, p2tog, purl to the end of the row.

Now decrease 1 stitch at the armhole edge on the next 8 (9, 11) right-side rows as follows:

Decrease row: K1, k2tog, work to the end of the row, and AT THE SAME TIME, continue to work decreases at the neck edge (knitwise or purlwise, depending on the row facing you, on knit rows knit to the last three stitches, k2tog, k1) on every third row 16 (14, 20) times, then every fourth row 2 (5, 1) times—18 (20, 21) stitches remain. Work even until the front matches the back to the beginning of the shoulder shaping, ending with the right side facing, 21 (22, 23)" total length.

Shape Shoulder

Bind off 7 (7, 8) stitches at the beginning of the next row. Purl the next row. Bind off 6 (7, 7) stitches at the beginning of the next row. Purl the next row. Bind off the remaining 5 (6, 6) stitches.

Right Front

With larger needles, cast on 57 (62, 67) stitches. Knit 6 rows in garter stitch (3 garter ridges). Change to cables and ladders pattern, repeat chart B across stitches for all sizes.

Work cables and ladders pattern until front measures 6½" (16.5cm) or your desired length for the border, ending with row 4 of the pattern. Knit another 4 rows in garter stitch (2 garter ridges), decreasing 4 (3, 3) stitches evenly across the last row as follows:

Decrease row: K11 (14, 16), k2tog, *k9 (14, 15), k2tog; repeat from * to last 11 (14, 15) stitches, knit to end—53 (59, 64) stitches.

Change to size 4 needles and continue in stockinette stitch until the Front measures the same as the Back to the armhole shaping.

Shape Armholes and Neck

Begin neck shaping at the beginning of the next (right-side) row, decrease 1 stitch by working k1, ssk, knit to the end of the row.

Bind off 9 (10, 11) stitches at the beginning of the next row. Now decrease 1 stitch at the armhole edge on the next 8 (9, 11) wrong-side rows as follows:

Decrease row: P1, p2tog, work to the end of the row, and AT THE SAME TIME continue to work decreases at the neck edge (knitwise or purlwise, depending on the row facing you, on purl rows purl to the last three stitches, p2tog, p1) on every third row 16 (14, 20) times, then every fourth row 2 (5, 1) times—18 (20, 21) stitches remain. Work even until the front matches the back to the beginning of the shoulder shaping, ending with the wrong side facing, 21 (22, 23)" total length.

Shape Shoulder

Bind off 7 (7, 8) stitches purlwise at the beginning of the next row. Knit the next row. Bind off 6 (7, 7) stitches at the beginning of the next row. Knit the next row. Bind off the remaining 5 (6, 6) stitches.

Sleeves (make 2)

With larger needles, cast on 47 (52, 57) stitches. Knit 6 rows in garter stitch (3 garter ridges). Begin cables and ladders pattern, repeating chart B across stitches for **sizes small and large** and chart A for **size medium**. Work 40 rows of the pattern repeat, ending with a row 4. Knit a further 4 rows of garter stitch (2 garter ridges), decreasing 1 stitch on the last row for sizes small and large as follows:

Decrease row: K22 (27), k2tog, knit to the end—46 (52, 56) stitches.

Change to smaller needles. Working in stockinette stitch, increase 1 stitch at each end of the row every 3 rows 12 times, then every 4 rows 12 times—94 (100, 104) stitches.

Increase row: K1, m1, knit to last stitch, m1, k1 on a knit row; on a purl row work p1, m1 purlwise, purl to last stitch, m1 purlwise, p1.

Continue in stockinette stitch until the piece measures 17½ (17½, 18)" (44.5 [44.5, 45.5]cm).

Shape Sleeve Caps

Bind off 9 (10, 11) stitches at the beginning of the next 2 rows. Decrease 1 stitch at each end of every row 13 (12, 9) times, then every 2 rows, 9 (11, 14) times. Bind off the remaining 32 (34, 36) stitches.

Finishing

Sew shoulder seams.

Front Band

Using the circular needle and with the right side facing, beginning at the lower Right Front edge, pick up 66 (68, 74) stitches from the Right Front, 55 (60, 62) stitches from the right neck shaping, 38 (40, 40) stitches across the back of the neck, 55 (60, 62) stitches down the left front neck edge, and 66 (68, 74) stitches down the Left Front. Work 5 rows of garter stitch, then mark the button placement on the left front band, and transfer this marker to the right front band for the buttonhole placement. On the sixth garter stitch row, knit to the first buttonhole marker, bind off 2 stitches, knit to the next marker, repeat the 2-stitch bind-off for each buttonhole you have marked. On the next row, cast on 2 stitches over the bound-off stitches. Work 2 more rows of garter stitch, bind off neatly.

Sew in Sleeves, sew sleeve and side seams. Sew on buttons opposite buttonholes.

Cassandra Cardigan Chart Key

☐ Knit on RS, purl on WS.

⊡ Purl on RS, knit on WS.

▷◁ C4F: Slip 2 stitches onto cable needle, hold to front, k2, k2 from cable needle.

Cables and Ladders – A

Multiple of 10 stitches + 2
6-row repeat

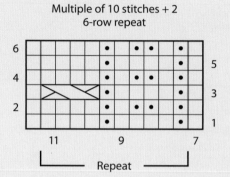

Repeat

Cables and Ladders – B

Multiple of 10 stitches + 2
6-row repeat

Repeat

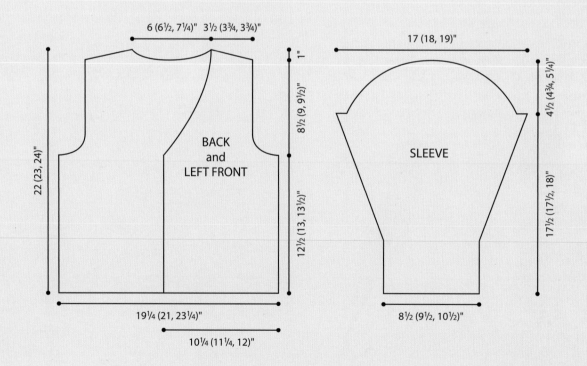

6 (6½, 7¼)"   3½ (3¾, 3¾)"

1"

8½ (9, 9½)"

22 (23, 24)"

BACK
and
LEFT FRONT

12½ (13, 13½)"

19¼ (21, 23¼)"

10¼ (11¼, 12)"

17 (18, 19)"

4½ (4¾, 5¼)"

SLEEVE

17½ (17½, 18)"

8½ (9½, 10½)"

Misty Meadow
Icelandics Farm

An Old-World Breed and
a New-World Approach

Minnetrista, Minnesota

*Newly sheared, an Icelandic sheep (opposite) at Misty Meadow Farm.
Above (clockwise from top left): natural fleeces, Icelandic lamb, felted wall
hanging by Judy McDowell, packaged roving.*

Ask Judy McDowell why her house is painted deep green with red doors, and she has a ready answer: "In Minnesota, you don't want a white house. It's sure a long winter." A native of St. Paul, born in 1959, Judy knows what she's talking about. Even in late spring, there are patches of snow on the ground, and buds don't appear on the trees here until May. But perhaps the house color scheme is a subtle indication that the McDowells, proprietors of Misty Meadow Icelandics Farm, actually like strong contrasts. After all, the tall, brown-haired city girl is married to a wiry, farm-bred boy, and that's "always been a good match," she says. Where the animals are concerned, "I don't tell Tom what to do."

For his part, Tom McDowell is quick to agree: "Our hobbies have complemented each other so well," he says, explaining how the farm suits his interest in raising sheep and his wife's passion for woolly crafts.

Although Judy's grandparents had been farmers in Sweden, when they immigrated to Minnesota, they moved to the city. "My parents' house was in an inner-tier suburb," she says, and "they never even did much gardening." And despite the nearness of farmers' fields, "my whole family,"

two older brothers and a younger sister, "feel like this"—Misty Meadow, that is—"is foreign to them."

Still the Swedish background meant there was a predisposition to doing things with your hands. Judy's father was a carpenter by avocation, and her mother was a painter and an avid seamstress. "My grandmother was a seamstress, too, and people "would come to the house all the time for fittings. I learned to sew from my mother and grandmother and then progressed on my own."

Looking back, she says she should have studied textiles in school. Instead she majored in communication and recreation at college. On the side, she apprenticed with a weaver, setting up the woman's loom and finishing off her projects. After graduation, Judy went to work for the Three Rivers Park District, beginning as an intern and staying in parks management and special events for twenty years. That's where she met her husband.

Tom's path to Minneapolis was more roundabout. Born in Chester County, Pennsylvania, in 1952, he grew up on his father's dairy farm. "We had sheep—Suffolks—for two years when I was in junior high school," he says, "and that's when I got my sheep experience." His understanding of

Tom McDowell (below) strolls a pasture with his flock. Opposite: Tom and his wife, Judy, share a sun tea moment on their front porch.

lambing, shearing, parasite control—it all dates back to those days. "My dad used to say you could take care of thirty sheep as easy as one cow."

Tom went to college in western Pennsylvania and taught high school biology in Virginia before joining the Peace Corps, which sent him to Belize in 1975.

"It was a great experience," he says fondly. "When my stint was over, I traveled in Central America and visited a lot of Mayan sites. I even learned to use a backstrap loom." One of his fellow Peace Corps workers had settled in the Twin Cities, and "I wanted to get out of the classroom," he explains. "It was the late '70s. My friend said there were jobs. So I packed my car and moved."

He went to work for the park district. Almost thirty years later, he is now the assistant superintendent, overseeing all programs and facilities, which include golf courses, ski areas, nature trails, and a cultural history center. When he encountered Judy in 1983, he was immediately struck by the textile connection.

"Tom said to me, 'You're apprenticing with a weaver?'" she remembers. His interest was piqued. A year later they were married.

In the late 1980s, the couple took a leave of absence and traveled for a year in Australia and New Zealand. "Wherever we went, there were sheep," Judy says. They began to talk about having a little farm.

Tom considers himself a passionate gardener, but he hadn't really dreamed of raising livestock, until, in 1989, they found an old alfalfa field twenty-five minutes west of Minneapolis. It had a tiny house on ten unfenced acres fringed by oaks, aspen, and maple trees. Suddenly sheep were a distinct possibility.

But first they had to come up with the name for the farm. "We did a chart of nouns and adjectives," Judy says, matching the words until they arrived at Misty Meadow. The phrase had the added resonance of being a phrase in a Moody Blues song, a plus for Tom, who is a fan of the group.

Finding the perfect sheep was slightly more difficult. "I wanted to do something different," Tom says. When he read that there were no Icelandic sheep in the United States, he thought he could be the first to have them. He contacted the Canadian woman who had imported some animals to North America but soon realized there were obstacles: "We didn't have a barn or a fence . . . and we had no money." It turned out to be a couple of years before they could go ahead with their plan.

By 1993, the McDowells had built a pole barn, thirty-two feet square, and they were finally ready. "We were the sixth or seventh flock in the United States," Tom says,

laughing that the flock consisted of one purebred ram lamb and one ewe.

Fifteen years later, the flock numbers about thirty—twenty-two ewes and eight rams—and Tom finds the animals as fascinating as ever.

Icelandic sheep are an ancient breed, he points out, "genetically the same as a thousand years ago," when the Vikings first brought them into Iceland. The animals still maintain a variety of colors and patterns in their fleece, from white to black and everything in between, and the ewes often have horns. Those qualities haven't been bred out, he says. "They also haven't bred the smarts out of them. In Iceland, they fend for themselves. They lamb on their own and have strong mothering qualities."

Another unusual feature is their double-coated fleece. The sheep have a long outercoat called a "tog," which was traditionally spun and woven into blankets and outerwear, and a shorter, softer undercoat, the "thel," which was used for garments close to the skin. The fleece can grow very long, Judy says, as much as eighteen inches a year, though Misty Meadow shears its flock twice a year to keep the fiber around eight to ten inches.

Icelandic sheep in the United States are still a rarity, but Tom widens the genetic base of his flock through a new artificial insemination process, with semen imported from Iceland. "They've done this with cows for years," he says,

An Icelandic ram (opposite) looks right at home in a grassy environment quite unlike its island of origin. Above: A tractor wheel piques a lamb's curiosity.

"but it wasn't possible with sheep till 2002, when a sheep scientist in Iceland began to develop the technique." Tom was one of a group of farmers who went to Iceland to visit the lab and learn about the procedure.

A second trip, though, came about almost by chance: "In 2003 we heard about a big Icelandair promotion at the Mall of America," Judy says. "They said there would be Icelandic horses, so Tom called up and asked if they would like to have Icelandic sheep, too. The organizers said yes." The McDowells walked three sheep right in through the mall and were rewarded with tickets to Iceland.

"The rugged, remote island was beautiful in a stark way," Judy says. And the experience of traveling there gave her a new perspective on the animals. "Here our sheep are so unusual," she says. You usually don't see anything like them in the United States. "But there you drive and see sheep everywhere . . . and they're our sheep."

The care of the animals falls to Tom, but it's clear that for him it's a labor of love. He usually gets up at six and heads for the barn, though the routine varies depending on the season. In Minnesota it gets cold in November, it's snowing a month later, and the white stuff sits on the ground till March, so "the animals spend the winter in the barn," Tom says. "But the doors are open about ten feet wide. If it's very cold or windy, I close them to three feet."

In winter, Tom puts hay in the fence feeders outdoors for the separate ewe and ram groups. "I check water troughs. I scoop grain to the chickens." The McDowells have half a dozen Icelandic and Araucana hens. "It takes fifteen or twenty minutes," he says. In lambing or breeding season he might begin slightly earlier.

In the evenings he follows the same routine: feeding sheep and collecting eggs, including the Araucanas' pretty green ones.

When the grass starts growing, Tom lets the sheep graze in the pastures, moving them every few days from one temporary paddock to the other. "This is a small hobby farm," he notes modestly, "but I want to keep it that size, so there's always good forage for the animals."

In summer there's not a lot to do, he adds, "other than lean on a fence post and soak it all in." That's more important than it sounds. The process of spending time watching the flock often reveals a great deal. "Are the sheep moving? Are they limping? Is anyone off by themselves? A lot is carryover from being raised on a farm," Tom says. "The piece that is intuitive is knowing what you're seeing, when to be concerned."

Tom handles most of his own vet work, including vaccinations and hoof trimming. And he breeds the sheep in the fall, using, in part, the artificial insemination technique. The lambs are born from April to May. "I love lambing season," Tom says. "I used to get up in the middle of the night, but I realized they do quite well on their own.

Linda Brodsky (in blue, above) joins the McDowells for a work-and-play session at the skirting table. Opposite: playing peek-a-boo in Judy's artfully felted wrist warmers.

Now I check on them at night and maybe get up early. Part of it is curiosity—I wanted to breed this ewe to this ram—and there's an element of suspense."

The lambs all get names, "though a couple of names are numbers," Tom jokes. They try to keep to an Icelandic theme, beginning each ewe line with the same letter. They'll sell most of the ewe lambs for breeding stock and take about five ram lambs to market. In Iceland, sheep farms emphasize meat, he notes, whereas "we were interested for the wool. But I tell people you can't get into raising them unless you deal with the meat."

Twice a year they shear the animals. "I've learned how to do it," Tom says, "though I'm not poetry in motion." Every fall they turn the occasion into a big event, inviting friends, fiber enthusiasts, and students to watch as Tom wrestles the sheep to the shearing floor. It's what keeps his five-foot-ten-inch frame so thin and strong, he says. He tells the visitors about the animals before turning them over to a professional shearer.

"We have hand spinners come," says Judy. "They pick up their fleece and put it on the skirting table," to clean it. "It's kind of like Tom Sawyer—they do all the work!"

Judy keeps a dozen fleeces to spin or use herself, then sends the rest to a mill to be carded into roving. "When I work with the fiber," she says, "I often think about Iceland—the glaciers and the glacial streams. There are no trees in Iceland. It's really different from Minnesota."

About eight years ago, the McDowells put a second story on their small Cape Cod house, the better to accommodate their family, which includes a daughter, Emily, now fifteen, and a thirteen-year-old son, Zack. A partly screened porch wraps around three sides, and inside, the furniture is a mix of antiques and mission-style tables, beds, and dressers.

"I have my felted rugs in the living room," Judy points out, "and some textiles on the wall. We're really into textiles—like molas from Panama"—and there are paintings, both works by local artists and others brought back from Australia.

The basement, which has huge windows that look out on the barn and sheep pasture, is home to Judy's studio. She has wool in plastic bins and baskets and crates stacked against the wall. Her loom is tucked away. "I talk about selling it," she notes, "but Tom says no." Several lightweight tables can be set up in varying configurations for small workshops or classes.

A few years ago, Judy left her job at the park department, and though she still does special writing and research projects, most of her time is spent working with fiber. She's usually in the studio, dressed in jeans and a sweater and perhaps one of her own felted wool scarves. Her interests have changed dramatically since she first apprenticed with the weaver.

"I didn't learn to knit till I was twenty-six," she says. "I tried to teach myself and couldn't get it right. Finally, I took a class. The teacher showed me a tension trick, and from then on, I couldn't stop. I was knitting up a storm."

After they moved to the farm, Judy taught herself to spin as well, to demonstrate what could be done with their fleeces. She'll spin for some customers, and she still knits for herself, keeping a dozen projects going at once.

"But in the last three years I fell in love with felt making," she says. "What's exciting is that it's an ancient technique used in a modern way. In 2004, she traveled to Wisconsin to study with Mehmet Girgic, a noted Turkish felt rug maker. "It's just a five-hour drive," she adds casually. "We spent three days making felt rugs." The next year she went back for five days to work on larger rugs.

Judy teaches felt making in her own studio but continues to learn from others, because, she says, "I feel like I'm discovering things all the time." One teacher came from Sweden and demonstrated techniques for three-dimensional objects, such as chickens in motion and puffins. It was a

little odd, Judy acknowledges, but it explains why her work space now includes an unfinished felt chicken and several felt rocks. "We wanted to see if we could do it," she says, enthusiastically describing how she experimented with putting colored felt moss on her felt rocks.

She tries to felt every day, getting into the studio around nine or ten, after dealing with correspondence, lesson plans, and other business. "I work five or six hours," she says, especially if she's doing production for shows and sales. She might concentrate on rugs or purses for two weeks then turn to scarves, which often incorporate hand-painted merino wool. "That gives it a watercolor look. I love it when my daughter comes down, sees something, and says, 'Can I wear that to school?'"

The McDowells have helped organize Shepherd's Harvest, an annual sheep and wool show that takes place in May. "And at the end of August there's the state fair," she says. "Thousands of people come, and we bring wool and felt. I get to stand and talk about wool and felting for twelve days straight. I really love it!"

There's plenty of opportunity throughout the rest of the year to exchange ideas with other fiber enthusiasts and craftspeople. She regularly meets with felters from the area. "We might share what we're working on and sources of supplies." Students contact her for workshops—on purses, hats, and wrist warmers, perhaps—and she'll go to other Midwest cities to teach, too.

"I'm also tied to an artists' group. We meet at each other's homes. There's a doll maker, a quilt maker, a bead worker, a paper maker, and a book binder," Judy says. "It's really inspiring to see things in other media."

The experience has prompted her to imagine new projects—like creating a large flat piece of fabric that she could cut and sew into a vest or skirt. And recently she's envisioned a more abstract work. "I've been going to the library and getting books about Matisse, thinking about his cutouts" and how to recreate them in felt. It would take a lot of time to compose, but the very thought has been exhilarating—even though "my son thinks I'm crazy," she says with a laugh.

Aesthetic judgments aside, Tom and Judy have made sure that their children were exposed to both the fiber and the livestock aspects of life at Misty Meadow.

"I think it's a great experience for kids to grow up around animals," says Tom, who still maintains some of the outlook of a former biology teacher. "They owned their own lambs and ewes when they were younger, and they've seen lambs being born. That's a special time—and a learning time. Besides, nothing is cuter than an Icelandic lamb."

Tonka Bay Tote

Designer: Judy McDowell

The geometric patterning and sophisticated palette on this bag are fiber artist Judy McDowell's signature. Once you've learned her wet felting method, you can improvise on this simple bag to create your own decorations with contrasting colored wools.

Skill Level
Easy

Size
One size

Finished Measurements
Bottom square: 12" x 12"
(30.5cm x 30.5cm)
Triangle: 12" (bottom) x 11" (side) x
11" (side) (30.5cm x 28cm x 28cm)

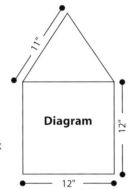

Diagram

11"

12"

12"

Materials
8 oz (227g) bar of soap (Judy likes to use an olive-oil-based soap because it softens your hands as you're working.)
Vegetable grater
1 gallon (4L) plastic container
Permanent marker
Bubble Wrap (resist material), 16" x 18" (40.5cm x 45.5cm)
Scissors
1 oz (28.5g) Harrisville Designs, 100% wool roving in color 7 Tundra for decoration
5 oz (142g) Misty Meadow, 100% Icelandic wool roving in natural black, for tote body
Sponges
Wastewater bucket
Piece of plastic window screen, cut to same size as pattern, 16" x 18" (40.5cm x 45.5cm)
¼ cup (60mL) vinegar

Preparation
Make the soap concentrate by grating the soap into the gallon container. Fill the container with warm water and let it sit overnight.

Make the felting solution by mixing 1 part soap concentrate to 8 parts water.

Make the Pattern
Using a permanent marker, draw a pattern on the Bubble Wrap to the dimensions specified above and cut it out.

Make a Prefelt
1. Divide the Harrisville Designs wool, for the decorative squares, into 3 even piles.
2. To lay out the wool, take 1 pile of wool and divide it into 6" (15cm) pieces. Hold one end of the roving in your right hand. With your left hand, hold down the end of the roving with the sides of your fingers and pull away gently with your right hand. You should have a thin layer of wool left on your work space. Continue to lay out the wool in this manner, overlapping wool like shingles on a roof until you have used one pile of wool. [Photo A]
3. Take the next pile and lay out the wool vertically.
4. Take another pile and lay out the wool horizontally.
5. To wet, pour felting solution over your hand so it spreads gently onto the fiber. Pouring directly creates dents. Wet the wool with felting solution, gently rubbing and patting until the felt forms. [Photo B]
6. Turn the piece over and continue rubbing and patting the second side. Do not felt too much—you just want the fibers to hold together. [Photo C]
7. Gently squeeze out the excess felting solution and set the piece aside.

Photo A

Photo B

Photo C

Lay Out the Wool

1. Divide the Icelandic wool for the tote bag body into 2 piles, one for each side of the tote. Set one pile aside.
2. Subdivide one of the piles into 4 even piles. Each of these piles will be used for one side of the tote.
3. Lay the resist pattern on your work space. You will be laying the wool directly on top of the pattern.
4. Using the 4 smaller piles you just created, lay 1 pile over the pattern horizontally, bringing the wool approximately 1½" (4cm) beyond the pattern. [Photo D]
5. Take the next pile and lay out the wool on top vertically. [See Photo A, page 63.]
6. Take another pile and lay on the wool horizontally.
7. Take the final pile and lay on the wool vertically.
8. Pat down and set aside.
9. Repeat steps 2 through 8 for the second pile. You now have two batts completed for the tote.

Photo D

Wet the Wool

1. Place one batt on your work table. This will be the back side of your tote.
2. Pour felting solution into the middle of the batt, making sure the edges stay dry.
3. Gently pat the wool to make sure that it is completely saturated, keeping edges dry.
4. Place the resist form in the middle and press down to get rid of air between the wool and the Bubble Wrap. [Photo E]
5. Gently coax the dry edges to fold over the resist form and into the middle of the tote. Make sure the wool is pressed firmly against the Bubble Wrap. Saturate the wool but do not begin to felt. [Photo F]
6. Place another batt on top.
7. Wet down the batt from the middle to the edges.
8. Pick up the entire piece from the top and quickly, but gently, flip over.
9. Wrap the dry edge pieces around the form, making sure that the fold is right up to the Bubble Wrap. Wet and pat down into the tote. [Photo G]

Photo E

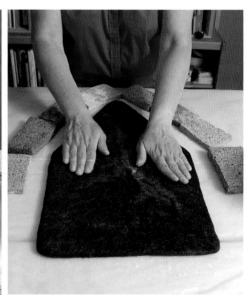

Photo F

Photo G

Felt the Tote

Begin the felting process by gently patting and rubbing the tote until the felt begins to form. [Photo G] The tote should be wet enough that your hands can glide over the wool. If this is not the case, you may need to add more felting solution or more soap.

Take care to work from the outside edges to the inside of the tote to prevent ridges from forming. When the fibers begin to hold together, press a little harder. Alternate between rubbing and pressing. As water comes out of the tote, soak it up with a sponge, squeeze it into the waste bucket, and add more felting solution to the tote.

Turn the tote over. This will be the front of your tote. Using the prefelt, cut squares approximately 1½" x 1½" (4cm x 4cm). Arrange the squares on the tote. [Photo H] Place the screen on top of the design. Add more soap mixture if necessary. Begin to felt, alternating between rubbing and pressing. Remember to start by working gently with the wool, increasing pressure as the fiber begins to hold together.

Cut the Strap, Felt Inside the Tote

1. Lay out the tote in front of you with the pointed end on top and the bottom of the tote closest to you.
2. Following the diagram on page 63, cut out the inner triangle piece at the top of the tote on both sides. Make sure that the strap is at least 2" (5cm) wide. [Photo I]
3. Gently rub the cut edges of the strap, taking care not to stretch the strap at this point. [Photo J]
4. Rub the cut edges at the top of the tote.
5. Carefully work your hand into the tote and start to gently rub against the inside of the tote. Work the edges all around to ensure the wool has begun to felt and there are no dry parts.
6. Carefully remove the resist form.
7. Continue to felt the inside of the tote, paying particular attention to the edges.

Full the Tote

1. When the fiber has begun to hold together, gradually increase pressure both inside and outside. [Photo K]
2. Continue to full until the tote is the desired size. Work in different directions to stimulate shrinkage in all directions. Coil up the tote and roll it back and forth on your work space.
3. Rinse in warm water until the rinse water runs clear.

Finishing

1. Soak in a vinegar rinse (¼ cup [60mL] vinegar to 1 gallon [4L] water) for 10–15 minutes.
2. Shape by placing the tote over a book covered in plastic wrap. Rub all sides so the tote conforms to the shape of the book. Air dry.

Photo H

Photo I

Photo J

Photo K

Kai Ranch

Inspired by History

Blue, Texas

Colorful Angora kids (opposite) wait in a Kai Ranch field. Above (clockwise from top left): natural-colored mohair yarn, woven fabrics by Lisa Shell, sign at the ranch entrance, shuttles wound with mohair.

Mohair on the move surrounds rancher and craftswoman Lisa Shell.

When Lisa Shell tries to explain how she became a weaver and breeder of Angora goats, she begins her story in Williamsburg, Virginia, where she was born in 1958. Her father was an innkeeper there when she was growing up, and her mother and grandmother worked as hostesses in the nearby re-created colonial village. She remembers watching, fascinated, as the weavers, spinners, and dyers interpreted and worked at eighteenth-century crafts. Wouldn't it be fun, she wondered, to do the same things herself one day?

The sheep that lived on the grounds of Colonial Williamsburg gave rise to another wish. Lisa decided she wanted to be the village shepherdess.

"I asked my mother to try to get me a job," she recalls. But Colonial Williamsburg said no. "They told her it wouldn't be authentic. The idea stuck in the back of my mind, though," along with the notion that it would be wonderful to live on a farm. Decades later, Lisa enjoys a hearty laugh over the way things have turned out.

For the past twenty years she and her husband, Randy, have made their home at Kai Ranch. The ranch, whose name means shell in Japanese, is located on thirty rural acres about an hour east of Austin, Texas. At any given time, Lisa raises between forty and eighty Angora goats, whose mohair she spins into yarn. She then weaves the yarn into shawls, rugs, and other silky soft creations. Goatherd, craftswoman, rancher . . . the people at Colonial Williamsburg should see her now.

The road to Kai Ranch was not without twists and turns. Lisa's father died when she was fifteen, and her mother remarried a few years later. Soon the family, including Lisa and her three siblings, moved to a farm in Georgia. "There were horses there, and it was a miraculous time for the whole family," she says. "Once that farm was under my fingernails, that was it!"

Even when she went off to college at the University of Tennessee at Chattanooga, Lisa commuted from a cabin on a farm in the woods in northwest Georgia, where she "was happy as a clam." She majored in anthropology—with a minor in biology to keep up her "interest in the natural world." And she met her husband, another student, working on an industrial archaeology project at the Chattanooga Choo Choo roundhouse, where one of their professors was leading an excavation. "We called ourselves educated ditch diggers," she remembers.

The couple married in 1981, and Randy joined the Air Force, which moved them briefly to Texas and then to Monterey, California. Lisa enrolled in Monterey Peninsula College, which offered an extensive crafts curriculum of weaving, spinning, and dyeing.

"Our dyeing class was in the home economics room," Lisa remembers. "Every stovetop was full of dye pots. I kept a dye notebook and had a blast." When the class took a field trip to a farm run by Anne Blinks, a noted weaver, textile collector, and founding breeder of naturally colored sheep in the United States, "I knew then that I wanted to learn more," she says.

And so when the Air Force transferred the couple to Okinawa in the mid-1980s, Lisa continued to work on her spinning. Over the three and a half years she lived on the island, she began teaching the craft to other military wives and a few local women as well.

While they were in Asia, the Shells had the opportunity to spend a month and a half in Australia, taking a working vacation on a sheep station in New South Wales. "We stayed on the ranch of the largest grower of colored sheep in the world and helped out during shearing," Lisa says. "We were roustabouts." The hard work convinced her that "no way did we want to raise sheep! We were blown away by what an undertaking it was."

The sojourn in Australia had also introduced Lisa to Angora goats. She had been fascinated by mohair since a spinning class in Monterey. "We were exposed to many different fibers, but it was the mohair that won me, heart and soul," she says, revealing an affection that has lasted some twenty-five years. "For me it surpassed all other fibers. Mohair is long-stapled, strong, lustrous, and easy to spin. And it took the dye intensely. I was amazed with its luster and silky feel."

Together with their ranching host in Australia, Lisa and Randy visited a breeder of colored Angora goats, which are far less common than the white variety, and many times rarer than their sheep counterparts. Lisa was fascinated by their rarity and their beauty, and soon after the Shells returned to the States, she began to seek out breeders who worked with the colored goats. Even so, and despite her reservations, the first fiber animals she owned were sheep.

The Shells were stationed west of Austin, in San Angelo, Texas, where Randy was an Air Force Chinese language instructor. The town called itself "the wool capital of the world" in those days, and sheep and goats filled the ranch pens for miles around. Thousands of animals were shipped out from San Angelo, and one day, as Lisa was driving down the highway, two sheep in the back of a trailer caught her eye—a moorit (brown) fine-wool ewe and a big black Karakul ram.

"I flagged the driver down and got him to pull off," she says, and told him she wanted to buy the pair. He turned out to be an order buyer, who bid at livestock auctions. Lisa got the two sheep and asked the buyer to keep an eye out for any odd-colored Angora goats that might come up for sale.

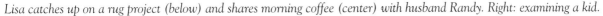

Lisa catches up on a rug project (below) and shares morning coffee (center) with husband Randy. Right: examining a kid.

Three months later the buyer had found ten animals for her: "They were not only colored but deeply colored—fire auburn red, deep chocolate, belted blacks, and solids. I took them all. I had to work as a flagger for a crop duster to pay for them, but I was finally on my way."

Two decades later the Shells are well established on their small ranch near the tiny town of Blue. "When you have livestock that graze, it's a ranch," she says, but adds that given the size of their property, the designation is "comical." Out of the military now, Randy works in child protective services for the state of Texas, and Lisa defines her job as "selling mohair on the hoof and off, in every state—from freshly shorn, scoured, carded, in roving, and in yarn."

The surrounding landscape of rolling hills is a mix of open and hardwood forest, with stands of yaupon holly that make much of the woods impossible to walk through. The neighbors aren't far, Lisa notes, but you can't see them for the trees. Ringed around a central area of open mesquite pasture—rather whimsically called the Lost Meadow—are several forests with equally colorful names.

"The boys have the Deep, Dark Forest," Lisa says. "The girls are in the Elm, Rain, and Magic Forests, or in the pasture." Patrolling the herd are two Great Pyrenees, whose booming barks keep other dogs and coyotes at bay.

Also on the land is an old goat barn, which the Shells are converting into a straw-bale house (an environmentally friendly design that uses bales of straw as insulation). "We're halfway done," says Lisa, with a quick sigh." It's a work in progress." Until it's finished, the Shells occupy a cozy yellow house with one big room for the kitchen and living room, with a separate bath and bedroom and a long screened-in porch. The home has wood floors and light green beadboard walls and is furnished with an eclectic mix of antiques and modern pieces, as well as "bits of things we've collected."

Along with the creative use of color, what marks the place as a craftswoman's home is the presence of art everywhere, beautiful pottery, in particular. "I've always had friends who were potters," Lisa says, "and I also swapped my work for textiles, prints, tiles, and quilts."

A nearby building, which also houses Randy's large, wide-ranging library, serves as her studio and retail space, though on chilly winter mornings when the fiber cannot be dried outdoors in the sun, the room most resembles a mohair warehouse. "There's fiber laid out on plastic bread trays everywhere," Lisa says.

The loom on which she weaves scarves, shawls, and lightweight rugs has pride of place in the center of the

A water trough turned sideways (opposite) keeps a delicate Angora kid out of the wind. Below: Lisa at the loom.

And who are the other garments for? Well, the goats, of course.

"This year the girls are wearing V-necks," she says. "On the guys a zipper front is preferable. It's not easy to dress a goat!"

Actually, the goats-in-sweaters look has less to do with fashion than with sound animal husbandry, beginning with the fact that Angora goats need to be shorn twice a year. "I shear in January," Lisa says, "so I can shear again in June. We get so hot in the summer here." But an Angora goat without a fleece is extremely vulnerable, she adds. They have to be kept out of the wind. They need a heat source or a covering. Since heating the barn would pose a fire hazard, Lisa's solution is to put the herd in sweaters.

Her shearing schedule is a constant in a roster of routine chores that shift with the seasons. "No two days are alike," Lisa explains, "other than I'll be feeding goats." The animals get daily hay and bag feed, and she moves them around from field to field, though there aren't a lot of paddocks to graze.

If the day-to-day work is open to various possibilities, the yearly chores are fairly predictable. Winter is the kidding season, especially busy for a rancher who does all her own vet work. "If it's a gorgeous day, the goats will kid in the pasture. But mostly they're in a pen, and I keep mother and kid there together for a day."

studio, and several spinning wheels bear witness to the hand-crafted yarn that fills the shelves and Shaker-style cabinets. Her huge rug loom has been disassembled, awaiting a move to the more spacious straw-bale house.

The studio is where Lisa spends mornings and evenings, wearing khakis in summer and fleecy sweats in winter. On chilly mornings she might put a warm cap over her dark shoulder-length hair and add a mohair sweater. Not one she's made, she's quick to add. "I've pretty much quit knitting. I'm more of a weaver. But I buy wool and mohair sweaters at thrift shops, go through the pile, and keep one for myself."

A frame holds the animal still as Lisa shears (below) and trims (right). Above: the latest in goat sweater fashion.

Hand dyeing locks of mohair (above) calls for thoroughly working in the color (center). The result adds elegance to a felt piece (right).

And there's shearing. Lisa used to hire a shearer, but in the mid-1990s she reduced her herd from nearly two hundred head down to a quarter of that number, in order to focus on producing the qualities she wanted in her animals—fiber fineness, good size, good mothering. After that she gave up the shearer and did the work herself.

"I learned a lot about the herd that way," she says. "I can shear as needed, and it helped me figure out what I wanted—and which animals to sell." She gives all the goats names because it's easier for her to keep track of names than numbers. And, besides, each animal has its own distinctive personality.

She currently has thirty does with kids, seven yearling does, thirty new kids, fourteen mature males, and a few retired animals. But to keep the herd numbers constant, and to obtain the most valuable fleece, it's necessary to sell about half the herd every year.

To understand why, it helps to know what constitutes the best mohair: "The finer it is, the more valuable it is," Lisa explains. And the very finest mohair is a kid's first fleece, known as "fall kid." "It traditionally went into men's suiting. The second, or 'spring kid clip,' is also valuable. Then there are two 'yearling clips.' After that, it is considered 'adult mohair,'" which tends to be used for women's sweaters and upholstery.

Lisa raises registered, show-quality animals, both colored Angora goats and white ones, whose very fine fleece is the result of generations of breeding. To develop the colored goats she wants, she tries to line-breed, or work with closely related animals. "You're trying to fix traits that are desirable," she says. "When it doesn't work, it's called inbreeding," she adds, with the characteristic wry humor that punctuates most of her conversations.

After the fleeces are shorn, they're scoured, or washed, and then carded. "I do the scouring and some sample carding, but most of the carding is handled by a carding mill." Similarly, Lisa hand spins about 30 percent of her mohair and sends the rest to a wool mill. "It depends on what I have and what I need," she says.

By the time spring rolls around, she's dyeing fiber. Along with vat dyeing, she uses some hand-applied color, after soaking the unspun mohair locks in a warm vinegary bath. Using three or four colors at a time, she'll paint the dye on and knead it in well. "I try to make sure there's color in every bit of lock. Then I steam it to set the color."

Every year Lisa's palette changes. "It depends on my mood and what I have in mind," she says. "Out here the brighter colors do very well, and it's fun to do avant-garde combinations. You may think you know what will come out of the dye pot, but you don't." The Southwest penchant for color—strong blues and greens—is very different from that of the East, where more subtle hues are prized. That's something she keeps in mind when she prepares for craft shows in other parts of the country.

Summer kicks off with another round of shearing, followed by "getting goats out on the road." Lisa delivers animals to her customers and attends an annual show held by colored-Angora-goat breeders. And when the weather begins to cool off, she participates in regional or national crafts shows, bringing fleeces, rugs, scarves, and shawls to sell. She'll include the work of other knitters in her booth and some crochet as well.

Lisa's been crocheting since a friend taught her the craft in college. But she only got as far as granny squares back then. Years later, when she needed a rug for her bathroom, Lisa remembered her grandmother's braided rugs

Lisa's weaving shows off the natural colors of her mohair fleece; a goat's horn provides a decorative cabinet detail.

and tried to achieve that same look through crochet. It was a good use of adult mohair, she discovered. "It feels so silky under your feet!" Her experience buying fleeces from others over the years has also given her insight into what other craftspeople want and need. "I save my best fleeces to show," she says. Her work has been recognized at the wool fairs in Taos and in Estes Park, Colorado, which have awarded her a string of blue ribbons.

In between the shows, there's mohair to be dyed, and weaving to be finished. "I don't start weaving till October," she notes, "and then I'm chained to the loom." With naturally colored mohair that's sometimes dyed to produce a heather effect, she might use a plain weave—an over-and-under pattern—to show off the yarn's qualities. "On a loom you've basically got a square, so I let color kind of 'walk' through the rug. I don't plot it out beforehand." The softness of the fiber gives the piece a rich feel. "I'll even put yearling mohair in the rug, for a really lush pile," she says.

Other projects might call for a diamond-twill weave, which rotates three colors of yarn to produce a diamond pattern. "The Navajos are known for their diamond-twill saddle blankets," Lisa says, adding that it takes more concentration to keep the pattern straight. "I can't talk to someone when I'm doing diamond twill."

Much of what she produces is sold at the Armadillo Christmas Bazaar, a popular local arts-and-music festival held in Austin every December. "It's my main show," she says, acknowledging that the craft show circuit can be exhausting. "It gets harder and harder. But once I get there, I love setting up a booth." And the contact with other artists often pays off in inspiration. "Basically we craftspeople are reclusive. This gets us out of our studio and into the world. I always come back with new ideas, and I'm reinvigorated."

Once a month, Lisa and a handful of other local fiber enthusiasts—dubbed the Blue Earth Guild—get together to knit, spin, and visit. "It's a very diverse group, and a lot of them are newbies to spinning." This is a way to share the fun of the craft. And once a year the guild comes over for a day of dyeing.

Other visitors also find their way to Kai Ranch. A few years ago, Texas mystery writer Susan Wittig Albert came calling. She thought a weaver would make an interesting focus for her series of plant-and-herb-based China Bayles whodunits. "She sought me out and interviewed me," Lisa remembers. The resulting mystery novel, built loosely on a fictional version of Lisa's work, was published as *Indigo Dying* in 2003.

But there's nothing made up about Lisa's love for what she does. "You have to be passionate about what you do," she insists. "This is for people who can't imagine doing anything else. And I can't see myself not raising goats."

From Turkey to Deep in the Heart of Texas

Naturally colored Angora goats are extremely rare, and the reasons stretch back millennia to the Biblical-era beginnings of the breed, in Ankara, Turkey. Originally the goats were small, probably around the size of a Border Collie, Lisa says. But as the demand for mohair rose after the Industrial Revolution, the Turks needed more fiber to sell. They crossed their Angora goats with larger, colored-fleece breeds to increase their animals' size, then bred the Angora goats back to white.

"When we see a colored Angora goat," Lisa says, "it's drawing on a recessive gene." And a rare recessive gene at that. Whereas about one in a hundred sheep are naturally colored, for goats the figure is one in five thousand. The fleece can come in a striking range of hues. "Think of human hair and all its colors," she says. "We'll get intense reds and chocolates on kids, but after a year the color lightens."

Angora goats were first imported into the United States in 1849, and by the 1880s there was a herd of more than seven thousand of them in Texas, where they were valued because of their ability to survive droughts. The numbers grew from there, especially around the Edwards Plateau in the west-central part of the state, where they could browse on live oak, even in dry conditions. The state became the world's number-one mohair grower.

And because the mohair market traditionally swung from high to low, the government installed an incentive program that was funded by a tax on fiber imported from other countries. At the peak of Texas production, ten thousand Angora goats were auctioned off each week at the stockyard sale barns in Junction, south of San Angelo. The program was cut off in the late 1980s, though, and the numbers of fiber-producing goats dropped off in favor of meat animals.

We're really not in goat country anymore," Lisa says. At Kai Ranch, however, they'll always have a place.

Angora goats make their way through a patch of yaupon holly.

Sage Brush Hot Pads

Designer: Lisa Shell

Simple crochet projects of richly hand dyed chunky mohair from Lisa Shell's studio become kitchenware that is art to behold on your pot rack or as fabulous housewarming gifts. All of Lisa's Mohair is hand dyed so ask about colors when you order the yarn.

Skill Level
Easy

Finished measurement
4¾" x 4¾" (12cm x 12cm)

Materials
Kai Ranch, 90% mohair, 10% wool, 3-ply, hand-dyed bulky yarn, 17 yrd (15.5), 1 oz (28.5g) in Desert Fire (square) and .5 oz (14g) each in Blue Bonnet and Sky Blue (round)

Size J-10 (6mm) crochet hook

Square Hot Pad

Foundation Round: Chain 5, join with a slip stitch to form a ring.

Round 1: Chain 3, work 2 double crochet in the ring, *chain 1, 3 double crochet in the ring; repeat from * twice more, chain 1, join with a slip stitch in third chain of starting chain-3.

Round 2: Slip stitch in each stitch to next chain-1 space, chain 3, (2 double crochet, chain 2, 3 double crochet) in same chain-1 space, *chain 1, (3 double crochet, chain 2, 3 double crochet) in next chain-1 space; repeat from * twice more, chain 1, join with slip stitch in third chain of starting chain-3.

Round 3: Slip stitch in each stitch to next chain-2 space, chain 3, (2 double crochet, chain 2, 3 double crochet) in same chain-1 space, *chain 1, 3 double crochet in next chain-1 space, chain 1, (3 double crochet, chain 2, 3 double crochet) in next chain-2 space; repeat from * twice more, chain 1, 3 double crochet in next chain-1 space, chain 1, join with slip stitch to third chain of starting chain-3; chain 6 for hanging loop, slip stitch in slip stitch just made. Fasten off.

Round Hot Pad

Foundation Round: Chain 5, join with a slip stitch to form a ring.

Round 1: Ch 1, work 8 single crochet in the ring; do not join the end of the round.

Round 2: Work 2 single crochet in each stitch around—16 single crochet.

Round 3: *Work 1 single crochet in next stitch, 2 single crochet in next stitch; repeat from * around—24 single crochet.

Round 4: *Work 1 single crochet in each of next 2 stitches, 2 single crochet in next stitch; repeat from * around—32 single crochet.

Round 5: *Work 1 single crochet in each of next 3 stitches, 2 single crochet in next stitch; repeat from * around—40 single crochet.

Round 6: *Work 1 single crochet in each of next 4 stitches, 2 single crochet in next stitch; repeat from * around—48 single crochet; slip stitch in next stitch, chain 8 for hanging loop, slip stitch in slip stitch just made.

Fasten off.

Shelves of Kai Ranch mohair yarns.

CHAPTER 6

Victory Ranch

Following the Unexpected Path

Mora, New Mexico

High on the appealing scale: alpacas (opposite) at Victory Ranch. Above (clockwise from top left): youngster in an alpaca shawl, ranch sign, hand-spun alpaca yarn on a pile of roving, spinning during a workshop.

Sometimes childhood dreams have a way of coming true. At least they did for Ken Weisner. "I always wanted to be a cowboy," he says. "Ever since I was four and I first saw Roy Rogers at the Armory in Chicago."

Ken wears a denim jacket over a plaid shirt and jeans as he sits in the store at Victory Ranch, drinking a cup of coffee at the round table that serves as a gathering place for employees and visitors alike. His thick watchband is studded with turquoise, and there's turquoise on his Victory belt buckle, too. His hair is surprisingly black for a man born in 1942, but much of the time it's covered by a black cowboy hat with a silver hatband of alpaca-shaped roundels.

Though Ken is rarely out riding the range, nevertheless he and his wife, Carol, have taken the eleven hundred-acre spread they bought here in Mora, New Mexico, in 1990, and turned it into the biggest alpaca ranch in the Southwest. The animals—smaller, finer-fleeced cousins of the llama—are visible grazing in the broad pastures that stretch away from the attractive complex of buildings at the center of the property. The alpacas are quite at home in this high country. The Mora Valley lies at seventy-two hundred feet, and to the northeast looms a snowcapped ridge of the Sangre de Cristo mountain range, where powdery rivulets hint that a late spring storm has just passed through. But then alpacas were originally bred in the fourteen thousand-foot-high Andes of South America.

Ken and Carol, on the other hand, hail from Midwestern flatlands, the South Side of Chicago, not far from Lake Michigan. "Ken and I have known each other all our lives," says Carol, who has on a red Victory Ranch sweatshirt and stretch pants and wireless glasses that darken in the sun. She and her husband interrupt each other frequently, bantering good-naturedly and correcting each other's stories as only long-married couples do.

"My father managed real estate"—apartments, she goes on, "and Ken's uncle supplied coal to those buildings. His cousin, Richie, was born a few days before me, so Richie was in my class. But the two of them were always together, so I knew Ken, too." She says they fell in love when they were ten. "I was the first girl he danced with at his bar mitzvah."

Things didn't go so smoothly after that, however. Carol went away to college and acquired another boyfriend. Until, that is, she transferred back to a school in the city and immediately bumped into Ken. Exit boyfriend. Enter married life and eventually two sons and a daughter.

Carol, Ken, and Darcy Weisner walk a pair of alpacas on the ranch.

Morning procession: Alpacas head far into the pasture.

Ken meanwhile went into business with his father. Together they bought a small auto wrecking yard and expanded it with notable success. (In fact, his company, Victory Auto Wrecking, has entered Chicago-area folklore for its television commercial, which has run on local stations more or less unchanged since the early 1980s.) But his cowboy idea hadn't completely faded. And there was also a decades-old connection to New Mexico.

When Carol was growing up, she went to summer camp in Michigan, where she and several close friends learned to ride. She loved it. "We got up at five to take care of the horses," she says, and went back every summer for five or six years, becoming good friends with the man who ran the horse concession, and his wife. "At fifteen, I was supposed to be a counselor, but the couple had moved to Las Vegas, New Mexico," about an hour northeast of Santa Fe.

"I took all my money, got on a train, and came to Las Vegas," she says. There she stayed with the couple and rode all summer. Through the years they all remained friends. "The first vacation Ken and I took was to Las Vegas, New Mexico," Carol remembers.

When Ken finally decided to look for a ranch of his own, the Weisners researched locations in several states. "But we realized we wanted to be here," in the Mora Valley, Carol says.

As luck would have it, they found the Old Rudolph Ranch, which had a gorgeous location on the "enchanted circle" of roads that lead to Taos and Angel Fire. The property extended up into hills covered by ponderosa pines, there was plentiful water in the old irrigation ditches, and large dirt-walled ponds were fed by runoff from the hills.

They weren't thinking about alpacas, however.

"I bought this place to raise cattle," Ken says, picking up the story. "But there was a downturn in the cattle market." He realized that if he wanted to keep the ranch, he'd have to look for something more profitable. Ostriches or emus were the initial candidates. Then, in 1991, a friend mentioned alpacas. The animals had been introduced to the United States just seven years earlier, when a small number were brought in to create a breeding herd.

"We didn't know anything about alpacas," Carol says.

"I didn't know anything about auto wrecking either," answers Ken.

They learned by the seat of their pants, they say now, making plenty of mistakes along the way. For example, there was the time they had an expert in to evaluate the herd. He pointed out what he considered their best animal—a wonderful male who could be a prize stud . . . if they hadn't just gelded it.

More than fifteen years later, the alpaca herd at Victory Ranch numbers 200 animals—about 125 hembras, or females, and about 75 machos, or males. They share the pastures with a few llamas, half a dozen horses (including a miniature stallion named Elvis), a couple of Border Collies, and nine impressive Great Pyrenees, who keep a watchful eye out for coyotes.

The alpacas are flat-out adorable—about three feet high at the shoulders, with fine fleeces that range from white and gray to multiple shades of brown and rich black. They're gentle animals, Carol notes. They have no top teeth, so when visitors hand-feed young alpacas, their nibbles simply tickle. Feeding is a highlight of the ranch tours that are offered several times a day. Most of the time a few cars pull up, carrying tourists bound for the ski resorts or families with youngsters who are fascinated by the gangly animals. But sometimes it's a busload of interested adults, like the social-work students from a nearby college who stopped by unexpectedly one day.

Carol gathers the visitors on the porch of the ranch store and fills in some background about alpacas and their close relatives—llamas, vicuñas, and guanacos. She talks

about how they breed and shear the animals on the ranch and explains a bit about the fiber. "Alpaca is thermal," she tells them. "It's lighter, softer, and warmer than wool, but you don't get overheated wearing it." Afterward she sits down to a spinning demonstration, then the students are turned loose to browse the store, get a closer look at the ranch, and hand-feed the animals if they wish.

The ranch itself is now a cohesive complex of buildings that look as though they came from the same architect and all went up at the same time. But that appearance is the result of a decade of improvements, and Ken seems to have an unending supply of projects for the future. The original dilapidated sway-roofed barn has been upgraded into a well-organized structure with stalls for the horses, covered enclosures for mothers and crias, as the babies are known, a tack room, and an office.

As for the inviting modern store, with its wraparound porch and accessible ramp, it's hard to believe it was once a ramshackle cinder-block box. But Ken proudly shows off the photograph that proves it, hanging near the front door.

There are also two houses on the property, a single-wide and a double-wide trailer that have been expanded, remodeled, and stuccoed to match all the other buildings.

The ranch's oldest structure is an old adobe house that Carol pegs at about seventy-five years old. "When we came, it had electricity," she says dryly, "a cord and a bare bulb." They thought about tearing it down but opted for a renovation instead. They left the original wood floors and thick walls, put in an office, a new kitchen, and several bedrooms. It's now a comfortable, convenient place for students of fiber arts to stay during workshops. Potential alpaca buyers also often spend a few days here getting a better idea of what it's like to take care of the animals.

Since 2000, it's been the Weisners' daughter, Darcy, who has overseen the day-to-day alpaca operation, with the aid of a ranch foreman and several other employees, while her parents shuttle among Victory Ranch, a house in California, and the auto wrecking business in Chicago, which their oldest son co-manages.

"I never thought I'd be doing this," the young woman says, brushing a strand of black hair away from her heart-shaped face. Thirty years old now, Darcy had studied fine arts in Boulder, Colorado, in the mid-1990s and worked summers at the ranch. "There were fewer alpacas then," she says. "After college I lived in the Bay Area for a while." But when the ranch manager left, she and her boyfriend,

Frequent visitors Jerome and Brianna Pacheco (opposite) cuddle an aging alpaca. Above: Knitter Dean Cheek works with barefoot confidence.

who'd been trained as an emergency medic in the Marines, came back to New Mexico to help out. "We were going to wait until they found the right person, but I really think there probably wasn't anyone better. I learned a lot. Now it would seem weird to live in Chicago or the Bay Area."

She's out by the barn early every morning watching closely as the mothers and crias leave the corral in an orderly parade, heading out to the pasture. The males are kept in bachelor herds in separate paddocks with their own small shelters on the other side of the ranch. The animals look delicate, but they're actually quite hardy, able to withstand both heat and cold. What's hardest on them, according to Ken, are warm humid nights and lack of sunshine, neither of which applies to the New Mexico climate.

"I make sure everyone looks ok," Darcy says about her routine, "and I check if there's anything that needs to be done, like grinding down teeth or hooves." She pitches in to muck out the corral each day, gives the animals shots, and worms them for the spring. She handles most of the other vet care, too, taking a homeopathic approach. And she keeps careful track of each alpaca. "They're DNA-tested and registered," she adds. There's lots of record keeping. "But really it's all about being aware."

"She can spot something early on, when you don't need much of a cure," notes Ken proudly.

"Alpacas are very smart animals," continues Darcy. "You have to develop a relationship with them." She clearly knows each and every animal, many of them since before their birth. "At first my dad was very involved in the breeding," she says. "Now he leaves it up to me."

The ranch has twenty stud males and has won its share of ribbons for prize animals. Still Darcy insists that breeding is hardly an exact science: "I can read about genetics like crazy—which for an art major is not an easy thing to do—

but sometimes you just throw your hands up in the air. Certain animals are predictable. Others you breed for ten years," and you get something different every time. "But the fiber is consistent," she says, "and our goal is healthy, quality-fibered animals."

They breed the alpacas over the spring, summer, and fall, and the crias are born eleven and a half months later, from June to October. The barn has pens where the mothers can give birth, but most of the time, Carol says, they have the babies in the pasture quite independently.

Each of the crias gets a name; Victory Ranch has a tradition of picking a different theme each year. There is one group with cowboy monikers, like Butch Cassidy, Maverick, and Dale Evans, and another named for famous people like Oprah, Humphrey (Bogart), or Miss Marilyn. One year they chose from a list of Italian foods, so there's a young alpaca named Fettucine Alfredo and another called Sambucco. It sounds a little funny, Carol admits, but the practice makes it easy to know how old each alpaca is.

After the crias are weaned, they're halter trained, sometimes by students during summer vacation.

Mid-June is shearing time. "We don't touch the fleece all year," Ken says, adding that the animals develop a crust that protects the fiber. "Before we shear, though, we'll spend a lot of time brushing them," then blowing out any remaining dirt. They set up a station in the barn, and a shearer from Colorado stays for a week, working through the entire herd. Each fleece is sorted, graded, and tagged with the animal's name before going to a hand spinner or to one of the mills that processes the long, fine alpaca fiber.

Besides selling the fiber, the ranch sells the animals as well. But the way they do it is unlike most other breeders, Carol emphasizes. They never sell them in an auction or over the Internet. "We want the crias to go to good people,"

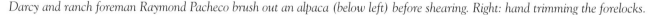

Darcy and ranch foreman Raymond Pacheco brush out an alpaca (below left) before shearing. Right: hand trimming the forelocks.

Carol examines newly hand-washed, mill-spun alpaca yarn.

she says, "so we offer good terms, and we board the animal for a year till the first cria is born." That way they can monitor the initial pregnancy and birthing situation. Then the animal is bred again, and mother and offspring go to the new owner.

"I follow the herds of people we sold alpacas to six years ago," Darcy adds. "When we sell them, it's a personal event."

Carol loves to upend a bag of fiber in the store and show the contents to visitors. "It's the same on the bottom as the top," she points out, passing out handfuls. Indeed, the alpaca fleece is as delicate and as varied as human hair.

Her interest in fiber came later in life. "My mother taught me to knit when I was five, but that was it," Carol says. "She was a wonderful knitter; I did doll clothes. When I met Kenny, I tried to knit him a sweater, but it came out too big. His blind grandmother told me how to fix it—just by touch!"

When they first started the ranch, she still wasn't very tactile, she says. "I couldn't tell the difference between soft and coarse fiber. Now I'm really good at it. A couple of years ago I heard the word 'weaving' on TV in another room, and I ran in to find out what the story was about. That's when I realized how much I'd changed."

The needlework hasn't improved too much, though. "I bought a book on knitting teddy bears," Carol says. "I thought that would be fun, and I could make one out of alpaca. I read the instructions wrong. It came out looking like a mouse," she says with a laugh.

She has learned to spin, both to demonstrate alpaca's wonderful qualities and to understand what craftspeople are looking for in the fleeces the ranch offers. She organizes the fiber workshops. There have been classes in spinning, knitting, weaving, and beading in the past. And she's commissioned other knitters to produce socks, sweaters, and children's and doll clothes for the shop. Other products, like luxurious capes and dyed baby alpaca yarns, are imported from Peru. But some of the most popular items remain the natural-colored, hand-spun Victory Ranch yarns, with each skein labeled with a picture of the animal it came from.

On a spring afternoon Carol takes time to walk through the pastures with a visitor, just to soak in the scenery and see what the herd is up to. "Every day is different," she says. "My friends from Chicago and California think we're out of our minds. But I love the quiet. I love the store. I love the animals. I love it all. I'm really proud that we know so much about alpacas. It's a far cry from being a Jewish girl in Chicago."

Meseta Alta Shawl

Designer: Dean Cheek

A simple lace pattern flows up the back of this triangular shawl. Knit in worsted-weight yarn, it is a great choice for a first lace project. Dean Cheek, the Taos-based designer, likes to knit the same pattern out of lighter-weight yarns, creating an airy, open shawl. Of course, dimensions will be different, so swatch first.

Skill Level
Easy/Intermediate

Size
One size

Finished (Blocked) Measurements
Top width, not including fringe: 77" (195.5cm)
Center length, not including fringe: 44" (112cm)
Long fringe: 7" (18cm)

Note
If you want a longer fringe, you will need to buy more yarn.

Materials

Victory Ranch, 100% alpaca, mill-spun, worsted-weight yarn, 798 yd (729.5m), 19 oz (538.5g) in Light Fawn (Victory Ranch sells their yarns by weight, wound off from bulk. Please order accordingly. Colors are natural fleece shades and vary from alpaca to alpaca.)

US size 9 (5.5mm) needles, or size needed to obtain gauge
Stitch markers
US size I-9 (5.5mm) crochet hook, for attaching fringe
7" (18cm) piece of cardboard

Gauge
16 stitches and 24 rows = 4" (10cm) in stockinette stitch

Special Abbreviation
Kfb: Knit into the front and back of the next stitch (to increase a stitch).

Shawl

Cast on 7 stitches. Work 2 rows in stockinette stitch, beginning with a knit row.

Next row and every following right-side row: Kfb, knit to the last stitch, kfb—9 stitches. Continue working this way until you have 21 stitches on the needle and the right side facing you for the next row.

Begin lace pattern: Kfb, k4, work row 1 of chart, k4, kfb. Continue working lace pattern as shown for rows 2–24 to set the lace panel up, then work lace repeat as shown above the red line on the chart, continuing to kfb at beginning and end of every right side row.

Repeat the chart from rows 25–56, 5 more times, then work 2 rows of stockinette stitch. Bind off.

Finishing

Block shawl by spraying it with room-temperature water and pinning it flat to dry, gently stretching it to open the lace section.
Wrap yarn for fringe around the cardboard and cut along one edge to create fringe strands. Attach the strands by using a crochet hook to loop pairs of strands through the shawl edge stitches, then fasten by pulling strand ends through the loops. When completed, evenly trim fringe ends.

Meseta Alta Shawl

Panel of 35 stitches
32-row repeat

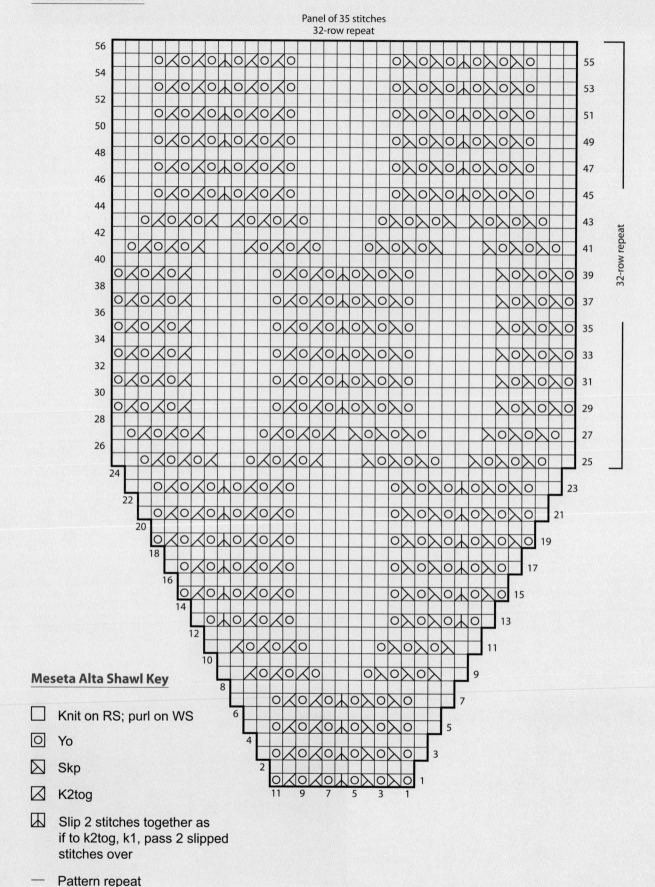

Meseta Alta Shawl Key

☐ Knit on RS; purl on WS

◻ Yo

⧅ Skp

⧄ K2tog

⧊ Slip 2 stitches together as if to k2tog, k1, pass 2 slipped stitches over

— Pattern repeat

Mariposa Cardigan

Designer: Dean Cheek

This sweetly cabled child's cardigan is named for Victory Ranch's favorite five-year-old fashionista. It is meant to be loose fitting and can be worn as a lightweight jacket, thanks to alpaca's amazing warmth.

Skill Level
Easy/Intermediate

Sizes
Child's Small/Medium (M/L)

Finished Measurements
Chest: 32 (36)" (81.5 [91.5]cm)
Length: 15 (17)" (38 [43]cm)

Materials
Victory Ranch, 100% alpaca, mill-spun, worsted-weight yarn, 664 (996) yd (607 [910.5]m), 16 (24) oz (453.5 [680.5]g), in natural white (*Victory Ranch sells their yarns by weight, wound off from bulk. Please order accordingly. Colors are natural fleece shades and will vary from alpaca to alpaca.*)

US size 7 (4.5mm) needles
US size 8 (5mm) needles, or size needed to obtain gauge
Cable needle
5 buttons, 3/4" (20mm) in diameter
Tapestry needle

Gauge
20 stitches and 24 rows = 4" (10cm) in main body cable pattern using size 8 needles

Special Abbreviation
Kfb: Knit into the front and back of the next stitch (to increase a stitch).

Cable Pattern for Back

Rows 1, 3, 7, and 9 (RS): K2, p1, *k4, p1; repeat from * to last 2 stitches, k2.

Rows 2, 4, 6, and 8 (WS): P2, k1, *p4, k1; repeat from * to last 2 stitches, p2.

Row 5 (RS): K2, p1, *slip 2 stitches onto a cable needle and hold to back, k2, k2 from the cable needle, p1, k4, p1; repeat from * to the last 2 stitches, k2.

Row 10 (WS): P2, *k1, p4, k1, slip 2 stitches onto a cable needle, hold to back, p2, p2 from the cable needle; repeat from * to the last 3 stitches, k1, p2.

Cable Pattern for Fronts

Work as for the Back, but begin and end each row k1 (or p1), instead of k2 (or p2).

Cable Pattern for Sleeves

Rows 1, 3, 7, and 9 (RS): (K1, p1) 4 times, *k4, p1; repeat from * 9 (11) times, (k1, p1) to last stitch, k1.

Rows 2, 4, 6, and 8 (WS): (P1, k1) 4 times, *p4, k1; repeat from * 9 (11) times, (p1, k1) to last stitch, p1.

Row 5 (RS): (K1, p1) 4 times, *slip 2 stitches onto a cable needle and hold to back, k2, k2 from the cable needle, p1, k4, p1; repeat from * 4 times, slip 2 stitches onto a cable needle and hold to back, k2, k2 from the cable needle, (p1, k1) 4 times.

Row 10 (WS): (P1, k1) 4 times, *p4, k1, slip 2 stitches onto a cable needle and hold to back, p2, p2 from the cable needle, k1; repeat from * 4 times, p4, (k1, p1) to the end.

Back

With smaller needles, cast on 69 (79) stitches. Work in k1, p1 rib for 5 rows.

Increase Row: Rib 4, *kfb in the next stitch, rib 5 (6); repeat from * to the last 5 stitches, kfb, rib 4—80 (90) stitches (1" [2.5cm]).

Change to larger needles and work the Back in cable pattern as given above until the piece measures 9 (10)" (23 [25.5cm]). Mark each end of this row with scraps of yarn for the underarm position. Continue in pattern until the piece measures 15 (17)" (38 [43cm]), then bind off all stitches.

Left Front

With smaller needles, cast on 34 (39) stitches. Work in k1, p1 rib for 5 rows.

Increase row: Rib 8 (9), *kfb, rib 6 (7); repeat from * to last 9 (10) stitches, kfb, rib to the end—38 (43) stitches (1" [2.5cm]).

Change to larger needles and work in cable pattern as given for Fronts until the piece measures 9 (10)" (23 [25.5cm]). Mark the right-hand end on right side of the last row with a scrap of yarn to denote underarm position.

Continue working even in cable pattern until the piece is 12¼ (14)" (31 [35.5]cm), ending with the wrong side facing for the next row.

Shape Neck

Bind off 7 stitches, work in pattern to the end. Decrease 1 stitch by working 2 stitches together at the neck edge on every other row 6 (8) times—25 (28) stitches remain. Work even until the Front matches the Back, then bind off all stitches.

Right Front

With smaller needles, cast on 34 (39) stitches. Work in k1, p1 rib for 5 rows.

Increase row: Rib 8 (9), *kfb, rib 6 (7); repeat from * to last 9 (10) stitches, kfb, rib to the end—38 (43) stitches (1" [2.5cm]).

Change to larger needles and work in cable pattern as given for Fronts until the piece measures 9 (10)" (23 [25.5cm]). Mark the left-hand end of the last row on right side with a scrap of yarn to denote underarm position.

Continue working even in cable pattern until the piece is 12¼ (14)" (31 [35.5]cm), ending with the right side facing for the next row.

Shape Neck

Bind off 7 stitches, work in pattern to the end. Decrease 1 stitch by working 2 stitches together at the neck edge on every other row 6 (8) times—25 (28) stitches remain. Work even until the Front matches the Back, then bind off all stitches.

Collar

Sew shoulder seams.

With smaller needles and the right side facing, pick up and knit 22 (25) stitches up the right front neck shaping, 26 (32) stitches across the back neck, and 22 (25) stitches down the left front neck shaping—70 (82) stitches.

Working back and forth in rows, slipping the first stitch of every row, work in k1, p1 rib for 6 rows or desired depth. Bind off loosely.

Button Band

With smaller needles and the right side facing, pick up 62 (70) stitches along the appropriate Front edge of the cardigan (Left Front for girls, Right Front for boys). Work in k1, p1 rib for 6 rows, ending with a right-side row. Bind off neatly in rib.

Buttonhole Band

With smaller needles and the right side facing, pick up 62 (70) stitches along the appropriate Front edge of the cardigan (Right Front for girls, Left Front for boys). Work in k1, p1 rib for 2 rows, ending with a right-side row.

Buttonhole Row 1: Rib 2, *bind off the next 2 stitches, rib 12 (14); repeat from * 3 more times, bind off the next 2 stitches, rib to the end of the row.

Buttonhole Row 2: Cast on 2 stitches over the 2 bound-off in the previous row. Work in k1, p1 rib for 2 rows, ending with a right-side row. Bind off neatly in rib.

Sleeves (make 2)

With larger needle and the right side facing, pick up and knit 60 (70) stitches at the armhole edge evenly between marked points on the Front and Back.

Begin cable pattern, and AT THE SAME TIME decrease 1 stitch by working 2 stitches together at each end of the fourth (eighth) and every following third row until 34 (38) stitches remain. Work even in cable pattern until the Sleeve measures 9 (13)" (23 [33]cm), ending on a right-side row

Change to smaller needles.

Decrease row (smaller size): *K5, k2tog; repeat from * twice, k6, k2tog, k 5, k2tog, knit to the end of the row—30 stitches remain.

Decrease row (larger size): *K6, k2tog; repeat from * 4 times, k6—34 stitches remain.

Both sizes: Work in k1, p1 rib for 6 rows, then bind off neatly in ribbing.

Finishing

Sew side and Sleeve seams. Weave in all the loose ends and block to size. Sew on buttons.

Mariposa Cardigan

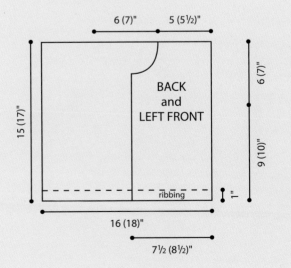

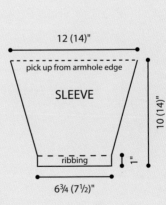

Taos Beret

Designer: Devra Wagner

An update on the classic beret, this hat features tiny cables surrounding the brim, and enough volume for an artful slouch. Designer Devra Wagner likes to top hers off with a vintage button. You can play with colors and stripes as you go, making the variations on this hat unlimited.

Skill Level
Easy

Size
One size

Finished Measurement
Circumference: 21"

Materials

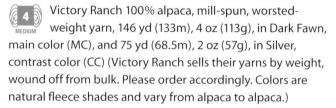 Victory Ranch 100% alpaca, mill-spun, worsted-weight yarn, 146 yd (133m), 4 oz (113g), in Dark Fawn, main color (MC), and 75 yd (68.5m), 2 oz (57g), in Silver, contrast color (CC) (Victory Ranch sells their yarns by weight, wound off from bulk. Please order accordingly. Colors are natural fleece shades and vary from alpaca to alpaca.)

US size 5 (3.75mm), 16" (40.5cm) long circular needle
US size 7 (4.5mm), 16" (40.5cm) long circular needle, or size needed to obtain gauge
US size 7 (4.5mm) double-pointed needles
Stitch markers
1 vintage button, approximately 1½" (4cm)
Tapestry needle

Gauge
20 stitches and 28 rows = 4" (10cm) in stockinette stitch, using size 7 needles

Baby Cable Rib

Row 1, 2, and 4: *K2, p2; repeat from * to end.
Row 3: *K2tog but do not slip from the needle, then knit into the front of the first stitch and slip both stitches off the needle together, p2; repeat from * to end.

Beret

With smaller needle and MC, cast on 108 stitches. Place a marker and join into a round, being careful not to twist the stitches. Work 8 rounds in baby cable rib.
Switch to the larger needle and knit 1 row, increasing 8 stitches by knitting into the front and back of the second stitch, and then front and back of every fourteenth stitch in the round—116 stitches. Knit 2 rounds.

Join CC at the beginning of the round and now knit every other row with CC for 1½" (4cm).

Knit 6 rows with MC, 3 rows CC, 3 rows MC, 3 rows CC; continue with MC until the work measures 6" (15cm) from the start of the beret.

Note
If you want to make the beret for a smaller head size, work this portion of the hat to measure 4" (10cm) instead of the measurement given above.

Next row: *K27, k2tog; repeat from * to the end of the round—112 stitches.

Crown

Note
Switch to the double-pointed needles when necessary.

Round 1: *K12, k2tog; repeat from * to the end—104 stitches.

Round 2 (and all other even-numbered rounds): Work even.
Round 3: *K11, k2tog; repeat from * to the end.
Round 5: *K10, k2tog; repeat from * to the end.
Round 7: *K9, k2tog; repeat from * to the end.
Round 9: *K8, k2tog; repeat from * to the end.

Break MC and use CC for the remainder of the beret.

Round 10: *K7, k2tog; repeat from * to the end.
Round 11: Knit.
Round 12: *K6, k2tog; repeat from * to the end.
Round 13: *K5, k2tog; repeat from * to the end.
Round 14: *K4, k2tog; repeat from * to the end.
Round 15: *K3, k2tog; repeat from * to the end.
Round 16: *K2, k2tog; repeat from * to the end.
Round 17: *K1, k2tog; repeat from * to the end.
Round 18: *K2tog; repeat from * to the end.

Draw the yarn through the remaining 10 stitches and pull tightly. Attach button and block. Weave in ends.

A Victory Ranch llama stands guard over grazing alpacas.

Lazy J Diamond Ranch

The Sheep Rancher as Storyteller

Rocky Ridge, Arizona

At Lazy J Diamond Ranch (opposite) the horizon extends to Little Black Spot Mountain. Above (clockwise from top left): weaving tools, Churro lamb, barnyard rooster, vegetal-dyed yarns.

t's only a few minutes, it seems, after Navajo sheep rancher Jay Begay Jr. has introduced himself to a visitor that he starts telling stories. He's a big young man, a bulky six foot two, with cropped black hair, a diamond-shaped face with prominent round cheeks, wire-rimmed glasses, and an apparently endless repertoire of legends, creation tales, and explanations that tie his surroundings and his daily life to traditional Navajo beliefs.

Among the very first things he shares is the story of how Talking God created the sheep. "He got the clouds," Jay begins, "and shaped the body. Willows became the legs. Rock crystals were eyes. The ears of the sheep were plants, and the rainbow made the horns and hooves. Then Talking God put the breath of life into the sheep. The elders tell us," he continues, "that if you have sheep you'll never go into hunger or poverty. It's the essence of our way of life."

And indeed sheep—for both meat and fiber—are the foundation of the Lazy J Diamond Ranch, which lies in the high desert of the Black Mesa region of the Navajo Reservation. It's a two-and-a-half-hour drive from the busy college town of Flagstaff, Arizona, on highways that decrease in size and traffic until, at the Rocky Ridge School, they turn to hard-packed sandy dirt that can be slick as ice when wet. After that it's another three miles to the long ranch driveway, where the Begays' robin-egg-blue house stands out against the tawny landscape.

The ranch setting has a timeless quality to it, accentuated by a subtly rolling panorama that stretches literally for miles in all directions, punctuated only by sparse piñon and juniper trees. From the house you can watch storms roll in and out and marvel at the play of late-afternoon sun on a distant flat-topped mountain. Remote as the place is, the ranch is connected firmly to the contemporary world, with cell phone service and satellite television reception.

At twenty-seven, Jay is young to be raising sheep. Most Navajos of his generation have turned to other occupations. But even when he was growing up, the animals fascinated him, says his mother, Helen. "He was interested in livestock since he was three, though we thought he was too small." He has certainly surmounted the difficulty of size. But Jay typically has his own traditional explanation for his path in life. "My umbilical cord was buried in a sheep corral," he says. That makes for a spiritual connection. This ranch is the home to which he'll always return.

Jay has learned the most about sheep and herding from his father's mother, Betty James Begay, who relied on her flock for food and fiber for the huge rugs she wove to support her eight children. Her lessons included the Navajo names for plants and which of those plants the sheep prefer at certain times of year. "She told me you don't just herd sheep with your eyes," he says.

Jay's mother's relatives—"all my relations," Helen interjects—were equally known for their animals. Before she was born, her grandfather, Cutfinger Smith, herded three or four hundred sheep in that same area. And Helen's mother, Sylvia Russell, was one of the last of her generation to raise Churros, the sheep closely associated with the Navajo people. "She would sell wool to weavers," Helen remembers, "and weave rugs that she would take to the trading post to sell for clothes and groceries. And she used to butcher sheep, so there was always mutton for us to eat. Some people say sheep are too much work, but I couldn't live without them."

One of seven siblings, Jay went to high school in Tuba City, boarding there during the week and returning home on weekends. He later got a liberal arts degree from Pima Community College in Tucson. Since then he has run the ranch with a passion. And he extends the same feeling to his work with Sheep Is Life, a nonprofit organization that promotes community education and outreach. Jay spends

Jay Begay spreads out dyed yarns and natural fleeces (left) on a sandstone ledge. Opposite: part of the Churro flock.

several days a week in the Window Rock office, organizing the group's annual celebration, educating tribal members about how to care for their sheep using a combination of Western and traditional methods, and helping the shepherds get additional value for their wool.

While Jay is away from the ranch, his mother cares for the livestock—his father, Jay Sr., works in Tuba City Monday through Friday—and his youngest brother, Michael, helps with herding. The modest, modern three-bedroom house is also the scene of frequent visits from an extended family. Younger sisters take a weekend break from school in Tucson or aunts pop in to gossip at dinnertime. An octogenarian great-aunt and her husband stop by to show a visitor a weaving sample. Jay's older brother and his wife, with their six-week-old baby laced snugly onto a wooden cradleboard, stay for a few weeks before they relocate to a town farther south.

Around the woodstove in the center of the living room, the conversation ebbs and flows in Navajo, punctuated by words and phrases in English. Among the surrounding books and the bric-a-brac, a few puzzling items call for an explanation. A long sheaf of straw on the wall turns out to be a traditional Navajo hairbrush, and a small flat basket cradles ceremonial feathers and fetishes. The two small pouches hanging by the front door hold cornmeal used in morning prayers—white cornmeal for the east, yellow for the west.

The rhythm of the day is governed mostly by the animals' needs. Along with a flock of about a hundred Churro sheep, the ranch is home to thirty to forty Angora goats, three horses, a few handsome roosters and a hen, countless cats, a young llama that's still learning its guard duties, and a half dozen dogs, including two Great Pyrenees. Cattle raised for meat roam the unfenced land, and for much of the day, the horses, sheep, and goats do, too. At night they return or are herded back to large corrals behind the house, carefully attended by the dogs.

On a brisk, windy spring morning, Helen ties a scarf over her long black hair and heads out toward the corrals. She whistles to the dogs and feeds them, then carries hay into a trough where the early lambs and their mothers are. The little ones hop right in with the feed.

"We help the sheep with hay in the winter," she says, "though if there's anything green growing, they'll go for

that. We might let them graze up into the mountains." In the summer—she gestures out in the other direction, where the land dips slightly—"we keep them down there, or we'll take them out in the valley on horseback." In the warmest months, the sheep are let out really early, so the animals get enough to eat by the time it gets hot. "They'll come back and stay under the trees and may go out to graze again at three till it's dark."

At the moment, though, the rams and the llama are in a separate part of the corral, and the pregnant females, both sheep and goats, are in yet another enclosure. For the pregnant animals, Helen puts hay in small clumps outside the fence, then opens the gate. According to some mysterious ovine sense of order, the ewes trot out first, followed by the does. A few new Angora kids are off in another small pen. They spring rambunctiously from corner to corner as Helen approaches.

The size of the flock depends on how much feed is available. "We used to have more sheep," Helen says, but during the previous year "it didn't really rain, and there wasn't much to graze." This year, with wetter weather, Jay plans to let the flock grow as more new lambs are born.

Later in the day, he checks on the sheep, whose fleeces are heavy and beautiful this time of year. The wool is white, gray, brown, and black, though up close the dark coats often look flecked with silver and the light ones have their own subtle variations. One badger-face lamb is marked with white around its eyes and a stripe down its nose; another has a panda face.

As he shows off the animals, Jay shares a traditional saying: "Mothers used to tell their daughters, 'I'm your mother, but I won't always be here. When I'm gone, the sheep will provide. They'll be your mother.'"

Jay laughs as he recalls traveling with his grandmother and how he used to "hate it when she said, 'Hurry, hurry. We have to get back to the sheep.' Now I'm the same way." As long as he can remember, the family always had a couple of Churros, along with Rambouillet sheep, the French and German descendents of Merinos. In those days, there was no good source to acquire more Churros, though the breed was always particularly well adapted to northern Arizona and New Mexico deserts. The animals can survive on less food and require less water than most other sheep.

"We went back into Churros in the '90s," Jay remembers, after the Navajo Sheep Project helped resuscitate the breed and bring animals back to Navajo herders. "Churros are hardy. They take hot summers and snowy winters, and they can lamb by themselves. The mothers are very protective." And their fleece, low in lanolin and easily dyed, can be spun without being washed first. It's especially good for the rugs, saddle blankets, and cinches that Navajo weavers are known for.

Jay usually shears his flock in April, though a few of the sheep and all the goats need to be shorn twice a year. He offers to demonstrate, picking out an impressive ram, grabbing a lasso, and circling the stiff rope over the ram's head in a move that evokes classic cowboy movies. Effortlessly hooking the ram by its horns, Jay leads the animal out of the corral and wrestles it onto its side on a large board in the yard. One of the dogs playfully tries to make off with the lasso, but Jay barely notices as he secures the ram's hooves with a sturdy wool rope, a hand-braided creation as beautiful as it is utilitarian.

"Before we had shearing scissors," Jay remarks, "they used to sharpen tin-can tops and use them." He has shears in a well-used workbox, however, and he wields them deftly,

Shearing a ram (below), Jay uses hand clippers (right).

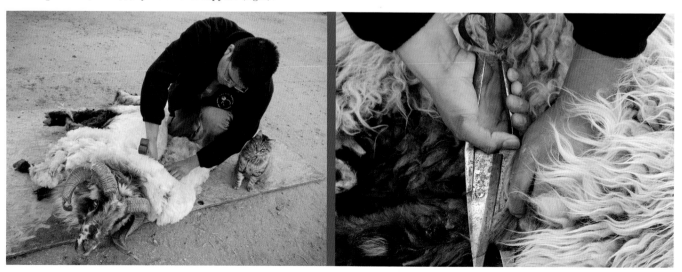

Weaver Rena Yazzie (left) explains a traditional storm pattern design; Helen Begay (right) restrains an obstreperous rooster. Center: neckline detail of a maiden's dress.

removing the ram's voluminous fleece as neatly as if he were removing a friend's winter jacket. Which, of course, is exactly what he's doing.

Though Churro sheep are capable of lambing twice a year, Jay breeds his animals only once, in late fall. Unlike other breeders, he tries not to select for twins, "because of the environment we live in. I usually tell people I breed for an all-around animal—color, fiber, conformation." The combination seems to be a winning one. Last year at the Churro association meeting in Flagstaff, both his ewe and his ram were named grand champions.

For Jay, the livestock shows and fairs liven up the summer months, and they're one of the reasons he often breeds early—"so the lambs will be big enough to exhibit at the first show in June." Mostly, though, he savors the opportunity to share his enthusiasm for Churro sheep. "I like interacting with people who have never seen or heard of this breed," he says. It's amazing to see people "become interested in the history."

Jay's house is full of fiber in every stage, from fleece to finished work, as well as tools to prepare it. A spinning wheel is propped against the living room wall, but he rarely uses it. He prefers the traditional Navajo spindle—a dowel with a disk near one end—that his mother taught him to use. From a plastic tub that sits next to the couch he pulls balls of various weights and textures of natural roving, as well as delicately colored skeins of yarn. He drapes the wool over his arm and talks about the vegetal dyes. For example, Navajo carrot and various lichens produce his subtle maize, teal, carrot, and olive hues.

"I especially like the dyeing," he says. "I started about six years ago, experimenting with the colors." He's also attended various wool workshops, both to teach what he knows and to learn other techniques, like felting. "They felted in the old days," he adds, "as lining for snow boots and for saddle blankets."

He sits down and attaches some roving to the spindle, rotating the dowel against his thigh and easily pulling the roving out into thread, which eventually wraps against the disk. There's a symbolic component to his actions, he explains: "The rod of the spindle is lightning," and the place the wool gathers stands for the earth. Because of this association with the elements, he puts the spindle aside when it begins to rain, only picking it up again when the storm has passed.

"You spin toward yourself," he adds, "because each sheep has a value, and you're bringing the value toward yourself." When Jay judges that the yarn is long enough, he three-plies it with an intricate movement of looping and stretching the strands, then spinning them together to produce a thicker yarn that he braids into rope or uses for the edge cords of a rug.

Jay's projects are everywhere, a tantalizing display of his talents. From a bookshelf, he picks up a finished horse's cinch he's woven in an intricate diamond twill pattern and recounts a legend about it.

"In the beginning of time, before humans," he says, pointing to a venerable slithery design, "insects, reptiles, and animals did all the weaving." The skunk produced the black-and-white pattern of chiefs' blankets, for example. But the great snake wasn't there. "The other animals went to him and asked him to do a pattern. He came up with this double-diamond twill."

Jay's upright loom stands in his bedroom, with a half-finished red-and-blue maiden's dress rising from the bottom. He shows how he moves the warp threads—the vertical ones—forward and back, using a hand-carved oak batten to hold them open. There's no heddle to pull the warp threads across. Instead Jay draws them through by hand, then flattens each row with a wooden comb.

Weaving is deeply rooted in Navajo tradition. Their creation stories tell how Spider Woman taught people the craft, using a loom that her husband, Spider Man, fashioned out of the sky and earth cords. But it's unusual for a Navajo man to weave. "I learned by watching my aunts and grandma," Jay says, "just watching and learning."

He's still mastering the ability to keep a pattern in his head. "A friend said I should make up a dance for it—like one step forward, two steps back." Mostly though, he says, "you have to think about the pattern from the middle. It comes from the center of your mind, and the warp has to be strong enough to hold your prayers."

Jay usually spins and weaves on weekends, but finding time is always a juggling act. Caring for the animals, keeping up the ranch, and trips and plans crowd his schedule. "We're thinking of taking the sheep up to Forest Lake this summer," he says. His grandmother had a sheep camp in the higher country there, and it's been years since anyone has used it. The grazing should be exceptionally good.

Jay maintains contacts with other craftspeople, breeders who have purchased his sheep, and those who have bought his yarn for knitting projects. And he has his own workshops to lead, as well as a wish list of future projects, like a double-faced saddle blanket with a cinch to match.

And as Churro sheep have become better known, the animals have been included in the Slow Food movement, which Jay has begun to participate in. In 2006, he attended the group's international conference in Italy, part of its efforts to recognize and promote heritage foods and breeds, from grapes and grains to cheeses and, yes, sheep. He has also provided animals for local chapters' special chef dinners, in an attempt to further extend the market for his Churros.

"Sometimes I think that because I love weaving and sheep, I'm in the wrong century," Jay muses. "But maybe not. My mother says you're not on this earth for nothing. You're here to make a change."

As he heads out into the twilight to feed his animals, Jay adds, "People ask why I do it. I say it's in my blood. My grandparents had sheep. If you're a Navajo, you're a sheepherder. That's who we are . . . shepherds and weavers."

Jay separates warp threads and, inch by inch, weaves a maiden's dress.

Back from the Brink

Descendents of the sheep that Spanish conquistadors introduced to the New World in the sixteenth century, Churros proved to be uniquely suited to the Southwest. The Navajo quickly embraced the animals, which provided meat, milk, and fiber known for its luster, natural colors, and durability.

In the old days, everything came from sheep, Jay says, and every part was used: "head, hooves, blood. Horns were made into rattles. Sinews were used for sewing." The animals also entered the tribe's spiritual life; a sheep song is part of the traditional Blessing Way and Beauty Way ceremonies. Elders taught that the sheep serve as protectors for a Navajo, Jay adds, shielding you "if someone wishes you harm. If a sheep dies, they say it stood in for you."

In the mid-nineteenth century, Army troops decimated the Navajo flocks as part of a military action. More recently, in the 1930s, drought conditions prompted the U.S. government to forcibly reduce the flocks still further. Those moves, and the introduction of other breeds—mostly Rambouillet sheep, which better conformed to East Coast ideas of what fiber should be—almost eradicated Churro sheep completely.

By the 1970s, there were fewer than 450 purebred animals left.

A veterinary scientist at Utah State University, Dr. Lyle McNeal, began to study the Churro, focusing on its genetic and cultural importance. In 1977, he founded the Navajo Sheep Project to find and save remaining members of the breed and eventually return them to Navajo sheepherders and Hispanic weavers. Along with students and volunteers, he scoured remote parts of the region, where animals had survived, and built a core flock in Logan, Utah. By 1982, the numbers had increased significantly enough that McNeal was able to start bringing animals back to the reservation in a program that continues to this day.

There are now more than eighty-five hundred Churros throughout the United States, including about five thousand on the Navajo reservation, where they are celebrated by groups like Dine ba 'iina (Navajo Lifeways) and Sheep Is Life.

Roping a Churro ram for shearing.

Hard Rock Snowboarder Sweater

Designer: Louann Kirkman with Mary Lou Egan

Louann Kirkman, a rancher with five radical snowboarding daughters, designed the first version of this sweater jacket. She knit it from bulky Churro yarn she spun herself. The double knit channels and longer shirttail were meant to protect her flying girls. Mary Lou Egan evolved the design into a wonderfully warm and stylish garment.

Skill Level
Intermediate/Experienced

Sizes
Women's Small (Medium, Large)

Finished Measurements
Chest: 39 (43, 47)" (99 [109, 119.5]cm)
Length: 20¾ (23¾, 26) (52.5 [60.5, 66]cm)

Note
You may adjust for length by following the section row counts for other sizes: small (5" [12.5cm]), medium (5½" [14cm]), large (6" [15cm])

Materials
Lazy J Diamond Churro, 100% wool, bulky yarn, 750 (875, 1,000) yd (686 [800, 915]m) in each color, dark brown and natural cream. (Order yarn by quantity needed; Jay's yarn is not sold in skeins.)

US size 15 (10mm), 32" (80cm) long circular needle
US size 15 (10mm), 16" (40cm) long circular needle
US size 11 (8mm) set of double-pointed needles
US size 10½ (6.5mm), 24" (60cm) long circular needle
Stitch markers
Stitch holders
2-way separating zipper, 26" (66cm) long

Gauge
8 stitches and 13 rows = 4" (10cm) in double knitting using size 15 needles and 2 strands of yarn held together
10 stitches and 14 rows = 4" (10cm) in stockinette stitch using size 15 needles and 2 strands of yarn held together

Special Techniques
DK: Double knitting
Kfb: Knit into the front and back of stitch.
Three-Needle Bind-Off: Hold front and back, right sides together. With a third needle, knit one stitch through the first stitch on both needles. Repeat, knitting a second stitch through the second stitch on both needles. Pull the first stitch knit over the second stitch. Continue across the row in this way until all stitches are bound off.

Notes
Counting stitches and rows in double knitting:
This pattern is written so that although there may be 18 stitches on the needle, I am only counting the 9 right-side knit stitches facing in the row counts, since they make up the right-side row. Row counts are also measured by the number of rows appearing on the right side of the work, not the actual number of rows knitted.

The sweater is worked with 2 strands held together throughout.

Right Front

With two strands held together and longer size 15 (18cm) needle, cast on 18 (20, 22) stitches.
With wrong side facing, purl 1 row.
Set-up row for double knitting: *Kfb; repeat from * to end—36 (40, 44) stitches

Double Knitting
Row 1 (WS): K1, *k1, yarn forward, slip next stitch purlwise with yarn in back; repeat from * to last stitch, ending k1. This row is repeated throughout.

Work a total of 28 (30, 32) rows (but counting as 14 [16, 18] rows on the right side. *See Notes.*)
Next row (WS): P1, *knit one stitch from front and one from back together (this closes off the first channel of double knitting); repeat from * across row, ending k1.
Row 16 (18, 20): Kfb into every stitch.
Repeat these rows once more, then work another 5 (7, 9) rows. At next row, begin armhole shaping, while continuing double knitting section.

Shape Armhole
Row 6 (8, 10) (WS): Bind off 1 stitch from the front and one stitch from the back together (this closes off the channel of double knitting at armhole) at the beginning of the next row, then 1 stitch in the same manner at the beginning of the 3 following wrong-side rows—5 bound-off stitches in total. Keep working the double knitting section pattern, keeping the edge stitches in stockinette for the remainder of the rows.

Row 15 (17, 19): P1, *k2tog; repeat from * across row, ending k1, p1.
Row 16 (18, 20): K1, *kfb; repeat from *, ending k1.

Work 8 (10, 12) rows in double knitting.

Shape Neckline
Row 9 (11, 13) (RS): Bind off by taking 1 stitch from the front and one stitch from the back together 2 (2, 3) times, (**this closes off the channel of double knitting at neckline**) work to the end of the row in DK.
Row 10 (12, 14): Work back in DK.
Row 11 (13, 15): Bind off 2 stitches, work to the end of the row in DK.
Row 12 (14, 16): Work back in DK.
Row 13 (15, 17): Bind off 1 stitch, work to the end of the row in DK.
Work even for 5 rows.
Note: This section will be 3 (5, 5) rows longer than the previous section.
Row 19 (23, 25): P1, *k2tog; repeat from * across row, ending k1, p1; put the stitches on a holder.

Left Front
With two strands held together and longer size 15 needle, cast on 18 (20, 22) stitches.
With wrong side facing, purl 1 row.
Set-up row for double knitting: *Kfb; repeat from * to end—36 (40, 44) stitches

Double Knitting
Row 1 (WS): K1, *k1, yarn forward, slip next stitch purlwise with yarn in back; repeat from * to last stitch, ending k1. This row is repeated throughout.

Work a total of 28 (30, 32) rows (but counting as 14 [16, 18] rows on the right side. *See Notes.*)
Next row (WS): P1, *knit one stitch from front and one from back together (**this closes off the first channel of double knitting**); repeat from * across row, ending k1.
Row 16 (18, 20): Kfb into every stitch.

Repeat these section rows once more, then work another 4 (5, 7) rows. At next row, begin armhole shaping, while continuing double knitting section.

Shape Armhole
Row 5 (7, 9) (RS): Bind off 1 stitch from the front and one stitch from the back together (this closes off the channel of double knitting at armhole) at the beginning of the row, then 1 stitch in the same manner at the beginning of the 3 following right-side rows—5 bound-off stitches total. Keep working the double knitting section pattern, keeping the edge stitches in stockinette for the remainder of the section rows.

Row 15 (17, 19): P1, *k2tog; repeat from * across row, ending k1, p1.
Row 16 (18, 20): K1, *kfb; repeat from *, ending k1.

Work 8 (10, 12) rows in double knitting.

Shape Neckline
Row 8 (10, 12) (WS): Bind off by taking 1 stitch from the front and one stitch from the back together 2 (2, 3) times, (**this closes off the channel of double knitting at neckline**) work to the end of the row in DK.
Row 9 (10, 13): Work back in DK.
Row 10 (12, 14): Bind off 2 stitches, work to the end of the row in DK.
Row 11 (13, 15): Work back in DK.
Row 12 (14, 16): Bind off 1 stitch, work to the end of the row in DK.
Work even for 5 rows.
Note: This section will be 3 (5, 5) rows longer than the previous section.
Row 19 (23, 25): P1, *k2tog; repeat from * across row, ending k1, p1; put the stitches on a holder.

Sleeves
Note
Sleeve is knit in stockinette stitch with 2 strands held together.

With double-pointed needles, cast on 24 (24, 26) stitches, join, being careful not to twist. Place a marker for the beginning of the round. Work in k1, p1 ribbing for 2½" (6.5cm).
Switch to shorter size 15 needle and continue in stockinette stitch (knit all rounds).
Knit 2 (2, 3) rounds.
Increase Round: K1, M1, knit until 1 stitch remains before the marker, M1, k1.
Repeat the increase round every other following round 0 (4, 5) times, then every fourth round 10 (9, 9) times—46 (52, 56) stitches total.
Beginning at the round marker, work even in stockinette stitch until the Sleeve measures 17½ (18, 18½)" (44.5 [45.5, 47]cm), or to desired length. Bind off all stitches.

Back
With longer size 15 needle, cast on 36 (40, 44) stitches.
Purl 1 row.
Set up row for double knitting: Kfb into every stitch—72 (80, 88) stitches total, 36 (40, 44) stitches facing when double knitting is worked.

Work double knitting as given for Fronts, working 22 (28, 34) rows in the first double knitting section only, working rows

3 (5, 7) as follows: Keeping in double knitting, knit into the front and back of the first and last stitches—39 (43, 47) facing stitches. *(The extra rows form a shirttail for the back.)*

Work as for the Front until the armhole shaping.

Shape Armhole
Bind off 2 stitches at the beginning of the next 2 rows. Bind off 1 stitch at the beginning of the next 2 rows 3 times— 5 bound-off stitches at each side total. Keep working in double knitting, keeping the edge stitches in stockinette for the remainder of the section rows.
Row 15 (17, 19): P1, *k2tog; repeat from * to last 2 stitches, end k1, p1.
Row 16 (18, 20): K1, *kfb; repeat from * to last 2 stitches, end k1.

Work 18 (22, 24) rows in double knitting.
Note: This section will be 3 (5, 5) rows longer than the previous section.

Shape Shoulders
Row 19 (23, 25): P1, *k2tog; repeat from * to last 2 stitches, end k1, p1. Mark the first and last 8 (10, 11) stitches for the shoulders, and center 13 (13, 15) for the Back neck. Leave stitches on a needle or holder.

Finishing

Join the Fronts to the Back at the shoulders using a three-needle bind-off.
Sew Sleeves into armholes using a single strand of yarn.

Sew the underarm seams from the wrong side using a single strand and an overcast stitch (mattress stitch makes it too bulky).

Neckband
Using two strands of yarn and shorter size 15 needle, beginning at the Right Front, pick up 8 stitches along the front neck, knit across the back neck stitches, pick up 8 stitches along the left side front neck—34 (34, 40) stitches. Work 1 row of k1, p1 rib.
Next row: Work in double knitting.
Continue in double knitting for a total of 9 right-side rows. Bind off in k1, p1 rib.

Zipper Band
On right front of sweater, with right side facing, using the size 10½ needle and a single strand of yarn, pick up 1 stitch in the front leg (side) of each of the stockinette stitches on the selvage. Purl next row. Knit 1 row. Bind off on the right side in purl. Repeat on left front of sweater.

Facing
On right front of sweater, with wrong side facing, using the size 10½ needle and a single strand of yarn, pick up 1 stitch in the back leg (side) of each of the stockinette stitches on the selvage. Purl 1 row. Knit 1 row. Bind off on the right side in purl. Repeat on left front of sweater.

Sew in the zipper between the band and the facing.

Hard Rock Snowboarder Sweater

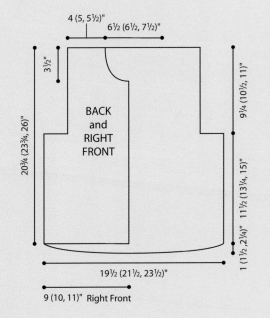

4 (5, 5½)"
6½ (6½, 7½)"
3½"
9¼ (10½, 11)"
BACK and RIGHT FRONT
20¾ (23¾, 26)"
11½ (13¾, 15)"
1 (1½, 2¼)"
19½ (21½, 23½)"
9 (10, 11)" Right Front

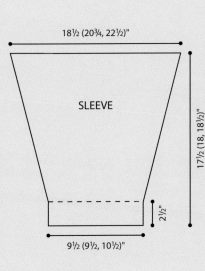

18½ (20¾, 22½)"
SLEEVE
17½ (18, 18½)"
2½"
9½ (9½, 10½)"

Navajo Braided Rope

Traditional

Jay Begay's hands are rarely idle. He grabs a lap spindle, spins lengths of Churro singles, and plies it in Navajo style, creating chunky yarn, all while chatting with visitors. This yarn is braided into thick, geometrically patterned rope. Jay learned this traditional braiding method from his elders. Although beautiful enough to hang on the wall as decoration, we quickly realized the ropes were made for function over form. We saw the ropes used as bridles on horses, as restraints securing a Churro ram's legs while shearing, and as cinches for keeping heavy objects in the back of a truck for a rough canyon ride.

If you want to give spinning a try, this is a good first project, as irregularities will be hidden in the braid. Or, start with purchased yarns and braid away. Once you've got the knack of it, you can create thick working ropes like Jay's or use lighter-weight yarn to make handles for tote bags or in place of I-cord in any knit project.

Skill Level
Easy

Size
One size

Finished Measurement
6' (2m) long

Materials

6 SUPER BULKY 12 yards (11m) each of Churro roving in color 1 (C1), shown in white, and color 2 (C2), shown in dark grey OR 12 yards each of 2 colors, in extra bulky weight yarn

¾" (20mm) round eye ring with a swivel spring clasp

Rope

Spin the roving and then 3-ply (Navajo ply) each color of roving. At the end of plying, you should have 4 yd (3.5m) of each color.

Put the strands through the ring so that you have 4 equal strands. [Fig. A]

Fasten the clasp onto something stable.

Fan the strands so that the 2 strands of C2 are on the outside and the 2 strands of C1 are on the inside.

Take the left-hand strand of C1, pull it around the left-hand strand of C2, and bring it back to the center. Make a knot with the other strand of C1, being careful to keep the left-hand strand on top [Fig. B]. Pull the knot snug. Move each C1 strand to the side, like arms. [Fig. C]

It's easiest to do the braiding if you are pulling the strands straight toward you, as if you are looking at the rope from the bottom. [Fig. D and E]

Knot the 2 C2 strands together, being careful to keep the right-hand strand on top this time [Fig. F]. Pull the knot snug. Move each C2 strand to the side, like arms.

Knot the C1 strands again, directly under the last knot, again keeping the left-hand strand on top.

Remember when knotting C1, the left-hand side is always on top. When knotting C2, the right-hand side is always on top. Pull every knot snug under the one above it.

The rope will form with each color in a separate line. [Fig G]

When you have completely braided the strands, knot them together to finish.

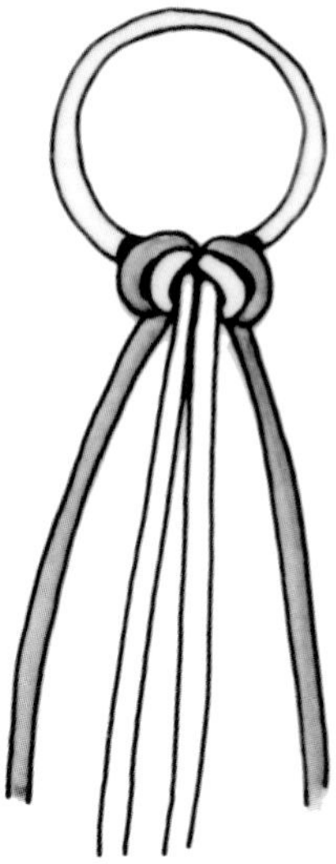

Fig. A

Fig. B

Fig. C

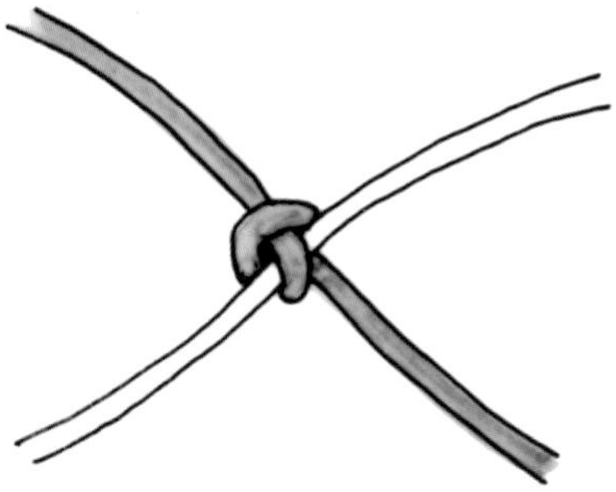

Fig. D
(Bottom view after colored knot)

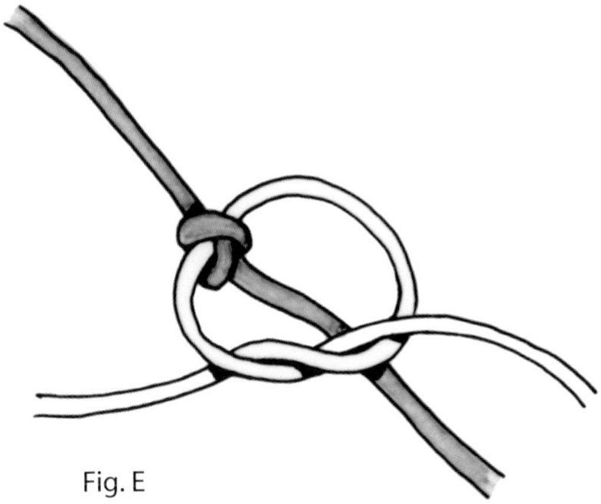

Fig. E
(Bottom view: white knot)

Fig. F

Fig. G

Illustration by Julie Fraenkel

Thirteen Mile Farm

Realizing a Vision, Acting on a Dream

Belgrade, Montana

Becky Weed (in shorts, opposite) and neighbor Molly Baxter cross a field below the Bridger Mountains. Above (clockwise from top left): lamb on alert, felted balls, deer horn button, knitting with Thirteen Mile Farm yarn.

There's no escaping the flow of the seasons at Thirteen Mile Farm, which sits in a spectacular valley in southwestern Montana. And for Dave Tyler, who owns the enterprise with his wife, Becky Weed, that's a good thing.

"The nice thing is the variety," he says on a day in late spring, when snow still tops the ten thousand-foot-high Bridger Mountains just a few miles away. "This time of year the grass is greening up, and I'm thinking of haying. But after six weeks, it's enough. I'm ready to put the machine away and move on to something else. The new lambs are fun," he adds. "They're jumping now, but it would drive you nuts if they did it all year."

In some ways Dave and Becky have applied that same to-everything-there-is-a-season approach to their own lives. Before they took on the challenges of a small-scale sheep operation, both of them had other careers in a different part of the country. Dave, who was born in upstate New York in 1943, attended the University of Maine as an undergraduate and "after several stops" wound up teaching civil engineering there, starting in 1972. He specialized in mapping, especially from aerial photos. "When I was a kid, I used to think I'd enjoy having animals, but my background was a long way from raising sheep. And I didn't know the word 'fiber' when I was a child."

Becky, sixteen years his junior, was born in Maine, where she continued to spend summers even after her family had moved out of state. A strong, slim, athletic woman, Becky says she was always happiest hiking in the mountains. And she loved to work with her hands. "I took a year between high school and college and worked as a carpenter," she says, but an interest in geology soon led her to study that subject at Harvard and, after graduation, to a job with the U.S. Geological Survey.

She worked on mapping assignments in California and Oregon but eventually returned to Maine and graduate school. One project even took her to Antarctica for a couple of months in 1982. "I was working with biologists

studying microorganisms," she remembers. That was where she got to know Dave, who was involved in another facet of the same program, charting the rate at which surface rocks were wearing away.

When he first met Becky, Dave recalls, she was already thinking about agriculture and land use, and as the two became a couple, they began to talk about "having land." The idea of owning a ranch grew out of that, and it "was one of the things we thought about, without ever believing that we'd do it." By June 1986 Becky had finished her master's degree, made three more trips to Antarctica (one was enough for Dave), and was ready to head west. Dave applied for a post at Montana State University, and when September rolled around, the two were living in Bozeman, where Becky had found work as an environmental consultant.

In Montana, the notion of owning land came naturally. The Gallatin Valley, at forty-six hundred feet above sea level, was gorgeous, Dave remembers, ringed by mountains and mostly agricultural in those days. "We wondered if we could have a ranch and raise animals. And could we eventually build it into a business?" They began to look for property and found what seemed like the perfect place—one of the oldest homesteads in the valley, with a log barn dating from 1864, a house built a year later, and numerous outbuildings on 160 well-watered acres, with cottonwoods growing along creek bottoms.

Ironically, the ranch had been established originally by a geologist who came West to pan gold in Virginia City, Montana. He and an adult son started adjacent ranches near Bozeman; his wife remained in Virginia City and did laundry for other miners, who paid her in gold dust, which the family used to buy cows.

By the time Becky and Dave saw the place, though, the house had been vacant for years. Even the "for sale" sign

Some of Thirteen Mile Farm's dyed yarns (opposite) atop weathered wood. Above: the farmhouse.

Dave Tyler rebuilds a fencepost (above) before turning to lamb chops (right) on the grill. Center: Becky with an armful of lamb.

was worn away and hanging askew. But the land was incredibly beautiful, Dave says. "We drove out and looked at the ranch and thought we probably couldn't afford it." When the real-estate agent told them the asking price, that suspicion was, unfortunately, confirmed. "Then the agent said, 'What about half the price?' I thought that would be insulting to offer," Dave adds, "but he said we should." The woman who owned the place had left it as a teenager and had just moved to a retirement home. With her family pressuring her to sell, she accepted the bid, and Dave and Becky moved in.

There was one more chapter, though, before they really settled into Thirteen Mile Farm for good. After three years at Montana State, Dave agreed to take a teaching job back at the University of Maine. It called for a five-year commitment. "We put the place on the market," Becky says, and she, too, went east to look for a job. However, the time in Montana had changed her. "I got off the plane and felt claustrophobic," she remembers. Instead of selling, they decided to rent out the ranch. Becky took a position in Colorado, and for the next four years the pair commuted back and forth in a long-distance marriage.

"Finally, in 1993, I came back to the ranch to put up fences," she says, "with the idea of working there full time." The next year, Dave also returned.

"I loved teaching," he says, "and I did it for twenty years." But he had always known he didn't want to do it forever. "I don't think engineering professors age gracefully." They don't turn into gray-haired sages. "The field moves fast; you're better when you're fresh. And I wanted to do something different when I was young enough to do it."

Dave now has gray hairs of his own, and a neatly trimmed graying beard as well, but he's still fast-moving. At six foot two, he's fit, friendly, and easygoing, as comfortable working on the farm's water system as doing the accounting or grilling a lamb steak on the barbecue. His skills and interests are complementary to Becky's, he says. "I'm better at keeping machinery running. I'd rather do that than call customers. And I'm not an expert at qualities of wool. Becky can sit down and produce a hat in a matter of minutes," he adds admiringly. "We'll be watching a movie, and she'll do a pair of mittens!"

Becky's ability to juggle several tasks at once seems as ingrained as her interest in fiber, particularly natural fiber, which goes back to her childhood. "I started young," she says. "My grandmother showed me how to knit." Then, when she was in high school, Becky also learned to spin and weave, though there were never enough hours in the day to keep up those hobbies. She also did some dyeing—gathering herbs and using them to color yarn. And she always liked creating things that were tangible, witness her skills as a carpenter.

Becky was less attracted to other aspects of farming. "It's the natural landscape that's most interesting to me," she says, not one that's plowed or sowed. And since this particular piece of land was best suited to grass, sheep seemed a logical fit. They "can be good for the land," she notes, "and you get great natural fiber." The couple has also had cows from time to time, both their own and herds they've pastured for others. "Mixing the species is good for grass management."

"I never wanted to do this as just a hobby," Dave adds, "and neither did Becky." One of their goals was to see if raising sheep on a small scale could be done profitably.

"Conventional wisdom says no," Dave acknowledges, "and frankly, it's not easy."

Still, they have persisted, and twenty years after they first bought Thirteen Mile Farm and more than a decade after they moved back to stay, the ranch and the business continue to evolve. The valley is as beautiful as ever. "It's bordered by faults," notes Becky with her geologist's eye, "so all the mountains are different." Trees and brush at the edge of their land create a contiguous pathway to a forest corridor for elk, coyotes, mountain lions, and birds, including migrating sandhill cranes. At the same time, the surrounding area has changed, undergoing a real-estate boom fueled by retirees and telecommuters. "This wasn't suburban in 1986," Dave says. "We didn't anticipate the development pressure in the valley. We couldn't afford to buy land now. It's been quite a transformation."

Over the years they've worked on the house, removing shingles and clapboard siding to reveal the original log construction, which was in surprisingly good shape for a dwelling more than a century old. Even the front door was still perfectly plumb, Becky discovered, when she replaced the old porch with a new one. Renovations also included turning two smaller rooms into a big open space with a wood stove in the center and an old stained glass window on one side. Bookcases line the walls, and woven pillows accent the oak mission-style furniture. And though Becky is self-deprecating about her decorating, it's a comfortable, inviting space.

For two people who had never managed a farm until they actually bought one, figuring out how to take care of the animals has been an ongoing process. "We didn't really know anything," Becky says candidly. "We read a lot and learned from the neighbors. We made a lot of mistakes." Dave adds, "It's been a somewhat steep learning curve. It's a business you learn every day."

And every day is different, they say, depending on the chores that need to be done and the requirements of the season. Becky's mornings are filled with phone calls, e-mails, and customers. She seems to run everywhere she goes, from snaking out a water system to picking colors for roving. Similarly, Dave might work on a solar-powered pump, then turn his attention to rebuilding a thousand feet of fence, readying the pastures before they bring in the sheep. In addition to their own acreage, they lease land from nearby farms to graze their flock, which now numbers

Thirteen Mile Farm raises sheep on a small scale . . . but in a majestic mountain landscape.

about 165 ewes, down from a peak of 300. And they both take care of the animals.

"We spend a lot of time feeding in winter and gathering hay in summer," Dave says. They move the animals around frequently. In winter, it's convenient to have them closer to the barn. In late spring the lambs and ewes might be in a pasture behind the house, while the rams remain in a separate pasture. Later, they'll shift the animals off to let the hay grow.

"Sheep don't want to be in the barn," says Becky, "though after shearing, they may come in. If the animals want to get out of the wind, they can get behind trees or other shelters." As part of the farm's predator-friendly philosophy, they rely on guard animals, first llamas, more recently a pair of dogs—a Great Pyrenees-Anatolian-Maremma cross—to protect the flock.

They breed the sheep in October. "We started with Corriedale," Becky says, "but have also used rams from several breeds—Border Leicester, Romeldale, Blue-Faced Leicester, Wensleydale. We don't strive for uniformity." What they do strive for is a good grass-fed meat breed with wool that makes for nice sweaters.

This goal requires Dave and Becky to pay close attention to the birth and fiber records of their breeding ewes. "We keep a database," Dave says, "but Becky carries a lot of it in her head. Ideally we'd want two lambs per ewe, but we don't achieve that. We raise the lambs till they're mature, then take them to be processed in Great Falls." The meat, which is certified organic, is sold to individuals, retail establishments, or restaurants. "Only in the last couple of years has wool gotten bigger than the meat business," says Dave. Now fiber is the main driver.

"I like long wools with a lot of luster," Becky says. And since more than half the flock has colored fleece, with different weights and textures, they have a variety of wool that can be used for different purposes.

The shearer usually arrives in March, and on shearing day, Becky and Dave reserve the nicest fleeces for hand spinners. Others they separate into categories by fineness and color—from varying shades of black to moorit (deep brown), grays, and white.

For years the wool went to a common wool pool, but gradually Becky became dissatisfied with that. "The price was low, and there was a penalty for anything not white and not fine." Later they tried having their wool processed into yarn, which they sold to hand knitters. But that, too, seemed unsatisfactory. The quality was not up to Becky's standards. "I knew the fiber could make nicer yarn," Becky says. And the dirt on the wool was valuable fertilizer, she realized, an asset they were giving up by having the fleeces handled elsewhere. Becky and Dave began to think about starting their own wool mill, and after visiting several, four years ago they took the plunge. They converted a white barn built in the late 1930s to a mill, attaching solar panels to the roof and installing a picker, a carder, a pin drifter to comb the wool, and a spinning frame. They recently added a second cottage-industry spinning frame as well.

"We knew in theory how the equipment was supposed to run," says Dave lightly, "but we didn't know much." Undaunted, they have enjoyed tackling the process.

Becky tends to express a more theoretical viewpoint. "Large-scale textile industries in the United States are dying

Lunch break at the mill (above): Mary Olson weaves a bowl, while Katey Plymesser knits a scarf. Top: Dave and Becky put out hay for cattle.

Katey concentrates on feeding fleece into the carding machine.

or dead," she says. "The way I view this, we're trying to address the question: can small-scale, decentralized agriculture and industry work? I'm curious, as fossil fuels become precious, is there a way to process closer to the source? The jury will be out for some time," she admits.

Inside the white barn, whirring, clinking, and whistling sounds fill the air. Katey Plymesser, who manages the mill, is wearing jeans and a sweatshirt and protection over her ears, as she works the machinery, which is simple in principle but still tricky to run.

Also a civil engineer by training, Katey moved to Montana in 2002 and only took up knitting in the last few years. She found she liked it so much she learned to spin and weave and now belongs to the local craft guilds. Researching a source for wool on the Internet, she discovered Becky, who lived just ten miles away. The two women connected, and in January 2006, Katey decided to give up designing water systems and roads for subdivisions and take on the challenge of running the mill. She splits the day-to-day tasks with a coworker, Mary Olson.

"Katey is twenty-nine and passionate about fiber," Becky says, "and she has an engineer's mind. She's always thinking about the system—figuring out costs and making the most of what's here."

"I like making the process more efficient," Katey says. "There's an environmental-political twist" to the work that "keeps me interested and makes me feel like I'm actually doing something about the environment." Occasionally she even finds herself giving tours.

"Today we had a hundred second-graders," she says, laughing. "And in the spring and summer people like to see the lambs and tour the mill. We show them the solar panels, and people want to see the dyeing." The dyeing, though, can be difficult to demonstrate.

On occasion Becky also works at the human-powered knitting machines, where she produces winter hats and custom sweaters. But in the future, Thirteen Mile plans to transition the knitting out of the mill and instead sell yarn to the Montana Sweater Company.

"The majority of our customers are from this region," Becky says, adding that they are set up to handle a variety of fleeces, including mohair, alpaca, and llama. "And we can do long fiber—from three to fourteen inches. That was a priority. Sheep go to all that trouble to grow long fiber; it's a shame to have to cut it."

Running the mill has been "fascinating but painful," Becky says, growing impassioned about how much most of us take manufacturing for granted. "This isn't unskilled labor, but society doesn't value it. We have to find customers who appreciate it."

Even with all the time spent on the mill, the animals, and simply keeping the ranch in running order, both Becky and Dave put in extra hours at board meetings and at nonprofit organizations. When Becky was recently appointed to the state livestock board for a six-year term, she entered "a whole new universe of state politics." And though she has left the academic world behind, she finds she still has to use her natural science background, as the board wrestles with issues such as the bison migration out of Yellowstone.

For his part, Dave is active in the Montana Conservation Voters and is a member of the Agricultural Development Council, which administers the state Growth Through Agriculture program. "It's a fund to support creative agriculture projects," he says. "We evaluate proposals and give grants and loans."

Above all, the pair tries to take advantage of the spectacular landscape that surrounds them. "This is a

hiking paradise," Dave says. "We can go in any direction, typically up in the mountains. We do cross-country skiing and sometimes downhill. There are lots of places to ski, and in winter Yellowstone is a favorite. If there's a frustration, it's that it's hard to get away."

And in autumn, they head even farther north. "Every September, religiously, we go canoeing in Canada," Becky says, "usually somewhere in the Northern Territories, where it's pretty remote." That's a way to recharge their energies and renew their enthusiasms. "It's odd that I went from being a natural scientist to this," Becky says. "I had a lot of jobs. Ranching is the hardest."

Becky and a colleague (below) plan a sweater from a swatch. Above: natural Thirteen Mile Farm yarns. Opposite: Max, a young guard dog, on duty.

Balancing Sheep with Native Species

Protecting flocks from the depredations of coyotes, foxes, mountain lions, and wolves can be difficult business in an area bordered by wilderness. But Thirteen Mile Farm has committed to predator-friendly certification, which means Becky and Dave choose not to use lethal controls like shooting, trapping, or poisoning.

"It's hard to lose animals," Becky says. Early on, when a coyote attacked their flock, they called in a government trapper. Neither she nor Dave liked that solution very much. They followed up by reading about guard animals such as llamas, which they used effectively for a decade, until the llamas suddenly lost interest. A year or so ago, they brought on a pair of Great Pyrenees-Anatolian-Maremma pups, which are growing into their guard duties.

Shortly after Becky returned to the ranch in 1993, a friend also told her about the predator-friendly movement, which was just beginning in Montana. "I went to a meeting," she remembers, "with a clothing manufacturer, a predator biologist, ranchers, and conservation people. They were interested in real issues, such as habitat preservation for wildlife and the preservation of rural economies."

In the last few years the idea has spread beyond the state, as Predator Friendly Inc., the organization that grew out of the early meetings, has begun to promote the idea of certification more widely and sign on a number of new ranches.

"The idea is as much about education of the consumer," Becky says, "as it is about providing alternatives for producers. We all have a lot to learn about the real costs of agriculture. And the group has helped tame the rhetoric between the agricultural community and the conservation community."

After all, she concludes, "If we can't learn to ranch with native animals, we shouldn't be ranchers."

Montana Tunic

Designer: Jennifer Olsson with Dee Grey

This loose-fitting tunic is more than a vest, less bulky than a sweater, and definitely not a poncho. Jennifer Olsson of the Montana Sweater Company has created a garment that perfectly captures the spirit of Thirteen Mile Farm: a functional, progressive, simple, and stylish piece that can go from a backwoods trail ride to lunch in Bozeman.

Skill Level
Easy

Sizes
Women's Small (Medium, Large, X-Large)

Finished Measurements
Chest: 38 (42, 46, 50)" (96.5 [106.5, 117, 127]cm)
Length: 24" (61cm) for all sizes

Materials
 3 (3, 4, 4) skeins Thirteen Mile Farm, 100% wool, sportweight yarn, 250 yd (228.5m), 3½ oz (99g) in gray heather

US size 6 (4mm) needles
US size 7 (4.5 mm) needles, or size needed to obtain gauge
US size 6 (4mm) circular needle, 30" (76cm) long
Stitch markers
Stitch holders
Tapestry needle
Two 1¼" (3cm) deer-horn buttons

Gauge
20 stitches and 28 rows = 4" (10cm) in stockinette stitch using size 7 needles

Special Abbreviations
1 x 1 Rib
Row 1 (RS): *K1, p1; repeat across row.
Row 2: Knit the knit stitches and purl the purl stitches as they face you.

2 x 1 Rib (multiple of 3 stitches plus 2)
Row 1 (WS): *P2, k1; repeat from * across to last 2 stitches, ending p2.
Row 2: Knit the knit stitches and purl the purl stitches as they face you.

Back

Note
The Back is shaped beginning at the underarm to allow extra room through the shoulder/back neck area; larger sizes do not have as much shaping as smaller sizes in order to keep the Sleeve cap from becoming too long.

With smaller needles, cast on 87 (97, 107, 117) stitches. Begin 1 x 1 rib, work even until the piece measures 4" (10cm) from the beginning, ending with a wrong-side row.

Change to larger needles and stockinette stitch. Work even until the piece measures 15½ (15, 14½, 14)" (39.5 [38, 37, 35.5]cm) from the beginning, ending with a wrong-side row; place a marker on each side for the beginning of the armhole (underarm).

Shape Armhole
Beginning this row, increase 1 stitch by working into the front and back of the first and last stitches of the row every 6 (8, 10, 16) rows 10 (8, 6, 4) times—107 (113, 119, 125) stitches. Work even until the piece measures 23" (58.5cm) from the beginning, ending with a wrong-side row.

Shape Shoulders
Bind off 7 (8, 11, 12) stitches at the beginning of the next 6 (2, 2, 6) rows, then 0 (9, 10, 0) stitches at beginning of the next 0 (4, 4, 0) rows for the shoulders—65 (61, 57, 53) stitches remain for the neck.
Place stitches on a holder.

Front

Note
The Front is worked without shaping.

Work as for the Back until the piece measures 5" (12.5cm) from the beginning (1" [2.5cm] above ribbing), ending with a wrong-side row; place a marker at each side of the center 39 stitches for pocket.

Pocket

Dividing Row (RS): Work across to the first marker; place worked stitches on a holder for the left Front, DO NOT cut yarn. Join a second ball of yarn and work across the center stitches; place the remaining stitches on a second holder for the right Front. Working on the 39 center stitches only, work even until the Pocket measures 5½" (14cm) from the dividing row, ending with a wrong-side row; place the Pocket stitches on a holder.

With the right side facing, return the stitches from the left Front holder to the needle; using the attached yarn, cast on 39 stitches for the pocket facing, then work across the stitches on the right Front holder—87 (97, 107, 117) stitches.

Work even until the Front measures 5½" (14cm) from the 39 cast-on stitches, ending with a wrong-side row; place a marker on each side of the center 39 stitches.

Joining Row (RS): Place stitches from pocket holder on a spare needle. Work across the left Front to the first marker; holding the Pocket section in front of the Front section, k2tog (1 stitch from the Pocket together with 1 stitch from the Pocket facing) across to the next marker to join the Pocket to the facing. Work even until the piece measures the same as the Back to underarm marker; place a marker on each side for the underarm, then work even until the piece measures 16" (40.5cm) from the beginning, ending with a wrong-side row; place a marker on each side of the center 45 stitches.

Shape Neck

With right side facing, work across to the first marker; join a second ball of yarn and bind off center stitches for the Front neck; work to the end—21 (26, 31, 36) stitches remain on each side. Working both sides at the same time, work even until the armhole measures the same as the Back to the shoulder shaping, ending with a wrong-side row.

Shape Shoulders

Work as for the Back.

Finishing

Block pieces to measurements. Sew the shoulder seams.

Collar

With right sides facing, using circular needle, and beginning at the corner of the bound-off stitches on the right Front, pick up and knit 52 stitches along the neck opening to the shoulder; knit across the stitches on the Back neck holder, decreasing 12 (8, 4, 0) stitches evenly across; pick up and knit 52 stitches from the shoulder and down the left Front to the corner of the bound-off stitches—157 stitches.
Work in 1 x 1 rib for 7" (18cm) from the pick-up row.
Bind off all stitches loosely in rib.

Sew the edges of the Collar to the bound off stitches of the Front neck, overlapping right over left.

Pocket Bands

With right sides facing and using smaller needles, pick up and knit 32 stitches along one side edge of the Pocket.
With wrong side facing, begin the 2 x 1 rib; work even until the band measures 1¼" (3cm) from the pick-up row.
Bind off all stitches loosely in rib.
Repeat for the opposite side of the Pocket.
With right side facing, sew the band ends neatly to the Front.
With wrong side facing, sew the cast-on stitches of the Pocket facing to the first row of the Pocket.

Side Bands

With right side facing and using the circular needle, begin at the lower left Front corner and pick up and knit 131 stitches evenly up the left Front, 1 stitch from the shoulder seam, and 131 stitches down the Back to the lower corner.
With wrong side facing, begin the 2 x 1 rib; work even until the band measures 2" (5cm) from the pick-up row.
Bind off all stitches loosely in rib.
Repeat for the opposite side.
Overlap the Front band on top of the Back band at the underarm marker, and sew together for 2" (5cm) through both thicknesses to define the waist.

Buttons

Attach buttons to the overlapped bands, at waist level, or as desired.

Using the tapestry needle, weave in the ends.

Business meeting at Thirteen Mile Farm (opposite): Becky and Jennifer Olsson of the Montana Sweater Company confer alfresco.

Montana Tunic

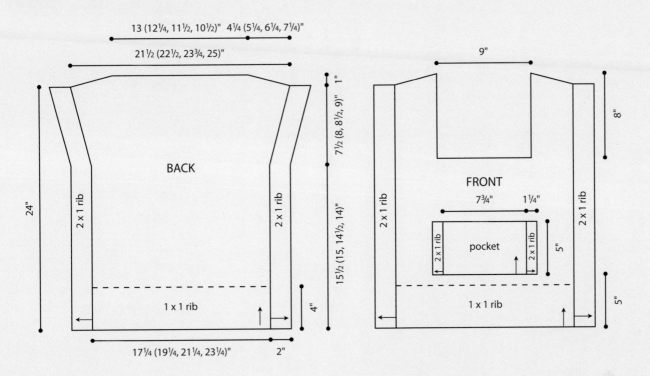

13 (12¼, 11½, 10½)" 4¼ (5¼, 6¼, 7¼)"

21½ (22½, 23¾, 25)"

1"

7½ (8, 8½, 9)"

24"

BACK

2 x 1 rib

2 x 1 rib

15½ (15, 14½, 14)"

1 x 1 rib

4"

17¼ (19¼, 21¼, 23¼)"

2"

9"

8"

FRONT

7¾" 1¼"

2 x 1 rib

2 x 1 rib

pocket

2 x 1 rib

2 x 1 rib

5"

5"

1 x 1 rib

Wolf Pack Hat

Designer: Mary Lou Egan

This hat, knit in the round, speaks to the predator-friendly philosophy of Thirteen Mile Farm. The lined brim keeps your ears extra warm.

Skill Level
Intermediate/Experienced

Size
Adult

Finished Measurements
Circumference: 21" (53.5cm)
Height: 9" (23cm)

Materials
 1 skein Thirteen Mile Farm, 100% wool, sportweight yarn, 200 yd (183m), 3½ oz (99g), in dark brown, main color (MC), 1 skein in tan, contrast color 1 (CC1), and 1 skein in medium brown, contrast color 2 (CC2)

2 US size 2 (2.75mm), 16" (40.5cm) long circular needles, or size needed to obtain gauge (one needle will be needed only for holding the hem stitches when working the joining round)
US size 3 (3.25mm) 16" (40.5cm) long circular needle
US size 3 (3.25mm) set of double-pointed needles
D-3 (3.25mm) crochet hook for provisional cast-on
Waste yarn

Gauge
25 stitches = 4" (10cm) in stockinette stitch using the size 2 needle

Hat

Cast on 144 stitches using a crochet (or other provisional) cast-on as follows:

With a smooth waste yarn, work a crochet chain about 150 stitches long. Starting 1 or 2 stitches in from the end of the chain and using CC1 and the smaller needle, pick up and knit 1 stitch in the back loop of each chain stitch until 144 stitches have been worked. Later, the chain will be unraveled and the resulting live stitches picked up to finish the hem facing.

Join into a round, being careful not to twist the stitches, and place a marker.

Knit rounds in stockinette stitch for 3" (7.5cm). Switch to MC. Knit 2 rounds. This forms the hem facing.

Turning Round

Purl all stitches. This will form a sharp fold line.
Using MC, knit 5 rounds.
Using CC1, knit 1 round.
Using CC2, knit 2 rounds.
Using CC1, knit 3 rounds.

Change to the larger needle.

Knit Wolf Chart

Some of the carries are quite long, so you may need to twist the light color behind the dark; these will be hidden by the hem facing. After the last row of the Wolf Chart is finished, change to the smaller needle for the next 6 rounds.

Using CC1, knit 4 rounds, using CC2, work 2 rounds.

Remove the waste yarn and place the live stitches on the extra 16" circular needle before working the joining round.

Joining Round

Fold facing along the fold line so wrong sides are together. Each stitch on the needle will line up with a stitch on the cast-on edge. With CC1, knit each stitch on the needle together with the corresponding stitch of the cast-on row.

The Hat is now worked on the larger needle. Following the Snowflake Chart, repeat chart 4 times, or to desired length. Break off CC1, and with MC begin decreasing for the top, changing to double-pointed needles when necessary.

Decrease Rounds

Round 1: *K2, k2tog; repeat from * to the end of the round—108 stitches.
Rounds 2 and 4: Work even.
Round 3: *K1, k2tog; repeat from * to the end of the round—72 stitches.
Rounds 5–7: *K2tog; repeat from * to the end of the round—36 stitches after round 5, 18 stitches after round 6, 9 stitches after round 7.

Finishing

Break off yarn, draw through the remaining stitches and fasten securely.
Weave in ends.

Wolf Pack Hat Key

■ MC
□ CC1

Snowflake Chart

Multiple of 6 stitches + 6
10-row repeat

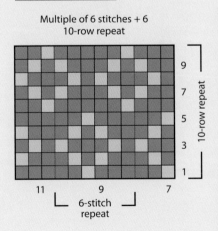

11   9   7

6-stitch repeat

10-row repeat

Wolf Chart

Multiple of 36 stitches

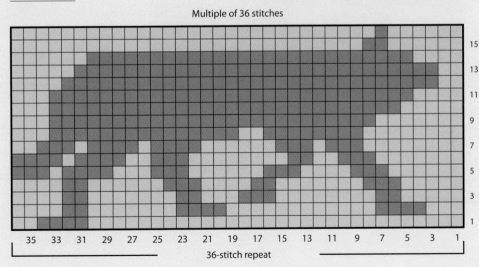

35 33 31 29 27 25 23 21 19 17 15 13 11 9 7 5 3 1

36-stitch repeat

Lars's Vest

Designer: Jennifer Olsson with Dee Grey

A simple, loose-fitting men's vest that looks great over flannel or denim. The deer tine embellishment lends it a Big Sky flavor that suits the natural yarns.

Skill Level
Easy

Sizes
Men's Small (Medium, Large, X-Large)

Finished Measurements
Chest: 38 (42, 46, 50)" (96.5 [106.5, 117, 127]cm)
Length: 25 (25½, 26, 27)" (63.5 [65, 66, 68.5]cm)

Materials
 3 (4, 4, 5) skeins Thirteen Mile Farm, 100% wool, worsted-weight yarn, 200 yd (183m), 3½ oz (99g) in Dark Chocolate

US size 7 (4.5mm) needles
US size 9 (5.5mm) needles, or size needed to obtain gauge
US size 7 (4.5mm), 16" (40cm) long circular needle for neck and armhole bands
Stitch markers
Tapestry needle
Deer tine with sewing holes for decoration

Gauge
18 stitches and 26 rows = 4" (10cm) in stockinette stitch, using size 9 needles

Back

Using smaller needles, cast on 76 (84, 94, 104) stitches.
Row 1 (RS): Work 4 rows in stockinette stitch, ending with a wrong-side row.
Begin k1, p1 ribbing; work even until the rib measures 2" (5cm) from the beginning, allowing the stockinette stitch edge to roll naturally and ending with a wrong-side row.

Change to larger needles and continue in stockinette stitch, working 2 rows even before starting the side shaping.

Shape Sides
Beginning with this row, increase 1 stitch on each side by working into the front and back of the first and last stitches of the row every 3 rows 5 times—86 (94, 104, 114) stitches. Work even until the piece measures 14 (14, 14, 15)" (35.5 [35.5, 35.5, 38]cm) from the beginning of the rib, ending with a wrong-side row.

Shape Armholes

Bind off 10 (12, 15, 18) stitches at the beginning of the next 2 rows—66 (70, 74, 78) stitches remain.

Work even until the armhole measures 8 (8½, 9, 9)" (20.5 [21.5, 23, 23]cm) from beginning of shaping, ending with a wrong-side row.

Shape Shoulders and Neck

Beginning this row, at the armhole edge, bind off 1 stitch at each side every other row 7 (6, 5, 3) times, then 2 stitches every other row 4 (5, 6, 8) times. AT THE SAME TIME, when the piece measures 10 (10½, 11, 11)" (25.5 [26.5, 28, 28]cm) from the beginning of the armhole shaping, ending with a wrong-side row, place a marker on each side of the center 28 (30, 32, 32) stitches for the neck.

Continuing shoulder shaping as established, work across to the first marker; join a second ball of yarn and bind off center stitches (between markers); work to end.

Working both sides at the same time, decrease 1 stitch by working 2 stitches together at the neck edge every row 4 times. Fasten off.

Front

Work as for the Back until the armhole measures 6½ (7, 7½, 7½)" (16.5 [18, 19, 19]cm) from the beginning of the armhole shaping, ending with a wrong-side row; place a marker between the 2 center stitches—66 (70, 74, 78) stitches remain; 33 (35, 37, 39) stitches on each side of the marker.

Shape Neck

Work across to the marker; join a second ball of yarn and work to the end. Working both sides at the same time, decrease 1 stitch at each neck edge by working 2 stitches together, every row 15 (17, 19, 20) times, then every other row 3 (2, 1, 0) times, and AT THE SAME TIME, when the armhole measures 8 (8½, 9, 9)" (20.5 [21.5, 23, 23]cm) ending with a wrong-side row, start shoulder shaping.

Shape Shoulders

Beginning this row, at the armhole edge, bind off 1 stitch at each side every other row 7 (6, 5, 3) times, then 2 stitches every other row 4 (5, 6, 8) times. Fasten off.

Finishing

Block the pieces to measurements. Sew the shoulder and side seams, matching shaping.

Neckband

With right side facing and using the circular needle, pick up and knit 100 (102, 104, 104) stitches around the neck edge. Work in stockinette stitch for 8 rounds, beginning with a purl round.

Bind off all stitches loosely.

Armhole Bands

Working as for the neck band, beginning at the underarm seam, pick up and knit 100 (108, 116, 124) stitches around the armhole.

Complete as for the neckband.

Using the tapestry needle, weave in ends. Sew deer tine at neck edge (see photo).

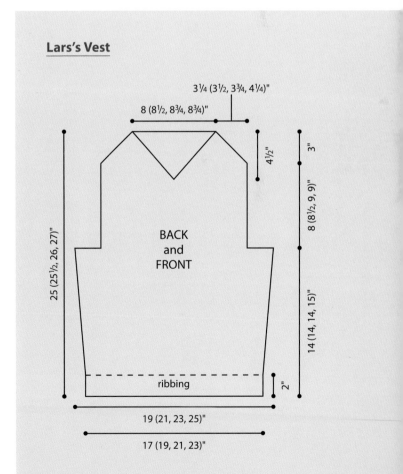

Lars's Vest

3¼ (3½, 3¾, 4¼)"

8 (8½, 8¾, 8¾)"

4½"

3"

8 (8½, 9, 9)"

25 (25½, 26, 27)"

BACK and FRONT

14 (14, 14, 15)"

ribbing

2"

19 (21, 23, 25)"

17 (19, 21, 23)"

Goat Knoll Farm

From Hobby to Business to Lifestyle

Dallas, Oregon

With snacks, Linda Fox (opposite) walks the herd to a Goat Knoll pasture. Above (clockwise from top left): a bounty of cashmere in the form of fiber on the hoof, dyed yarn, roving, and a knitted swatch.

When the treasurer/tax collector of Polk County, Oregon, takes a break for lunch, she usually doesn't head for a local restaurant. Instead, on warm days, Linda Fox often walks out of the imposing brick courthouse in the center of Dallas, in the Willamette Valley, gets on her bicycle, and pedals a mile or so up the hill to Goat Knoll Farm. There she'll have a bite of food at the contemporary-style farmhouse she shares with her husband, Paul Johnson. Before returning to her job as an elected public official, she lingers a moment to pet the cat and then checks the goats and sheep in the pastures. It's a pleasant interlude in a busy day, just one way Linda and Paul integrate their professional selves with the routine of running a fifty-acre farm.

Neither Paul nor Linda is exactly a stranger to rural life. Paul was born in Nebraska, in a town of eight hundred people, almost sixty-one years ago. "Growing up I had jobs taking care of livestock," he says, adding with the dry irony that colors his conversation, "I swore then I'd never live on a farm."

Linda, who is five years younger than Paul, is a native of Elmira, Oregon, where she grew up with five brothers and sisters. "We're just an hour from where I was born," she says. "My father worked in a plywood mill. But we had forty acres and raised our own food. For six kids, that was important."

There were chickens for eating and eggs, occasionally rabbits, and a dairy cow whose calves provided meat for the family.

Education and jobs took Paul and Linda in different directions. Paul started college in Nebraska, went to school in Denver, and worked in accounting and then in labor relations, moving from Colorado to northern California to Oklahoma then Arizona in the course of his career. Married and divorced, he was offered a position in Oregon in 1991, which is when he moved to Portland.

"I was president of an employers' association for ten years," he says. "I did community mediation in Polk County—dog cases and runaway children, for instance—and was a state mediator for three years." He still serves as a mediator and labor negotiator, though now he mostly works from home.

Linda studied computer programming and accounting in Oregon. When she realized that a computer position would mean a move to California, she became a CPA instead. "I owned my own public accounting firm for twenty years," she says.

She, too, was married previously, and in 1978 she and her first husband bought the property in Dallas. They lived there for a while, trying out the country lifestyle. They boarded horses and kept chickens and dairy goats as well.

Linda coaxes a reluctant goat (opposite) through a doorway. Below: She and her husband, Paul Johnson, visit with the kids in the barnyard.

A hug for a kid (above); Paul talks with Worf, the farm's oldest buck (right).

"We were experimenting," Linda recalls. "We even tried making goat cheese—not very successfully," she adds with a rueful laugh.

When Linda and her husband divorced, she kept the farm, renting out the old house while she lived and worked in Portland. Her office was in the same building as Paul's. He first spotted her, he jokes, when he went for a smoke in the courtyard outside the women's restroom, though he's quick to point out that he's since given up cigarettes. When they actually met, Paul and Linda realized the chemistry was there, along with a shared penchant for unconventional settings. Two years later, Paul says, "We got married at the bottom of the Grand Canyon."

Little by little the couple began to share their lives with animals. They moved to Tigard, southwest of Portland, to a home on two acres. "It came with two chickens, two geese, one old goat, and one old sheep," Linda says. She and Paul soon discovered they wanted more.

The Internet was not yet as popular as it is now, but as self-described computer nerds, the two were able to search online for different kinds of livestock. "We ran across articles on cashmere goats," Paul remembers. The idea of goats was appealing, particularly those that didn't have to be milked twice a day. And by the early 1990s, more than a decade after the first cashmere goats were imported into the United States, the exotic appeal of the animals had dwindled and their high cost had returned to a more reasonable level. "The prices were just goat prices," Paul says. So in 1994, he and Linda bought three. They have never regretted it.

"Goats are a lot of fun," Paul explains, "and they're intelligent. With sheep I feel superior. But with goats . . . I'm about even."

More than a decade later, all the signs were pointing toward a move to Dallas. Linda's farm renters moved out, and she and Paul began staying at the farm on weekends. It's a beautiful spot, forty-five miles from the Pacific, at the edge of the Coast Range. The town of fourteen thousand has become a bedroom community for Salem, Oregon's capital, but as Linda notes, you get rural really fast.

The surrounding hills are green with firs and oaks, and on a clear day you may even see the Cascades. The farm, though, was not in pristine condition. "The land was a sea of wild blackberries," Paul says. Clearly more goats were needed to rid the land of the overgrowth.

The prudent thing would have been to build a fence when the time was right and then look for the animals. But prudence isn't always an option. One day "someone offered us a herd of forty-one goats," Paul says, "and we made a decision: We'll just move to the old place. We had three weeks to put up a fence and turn the garage into a barn. The goats cleared the property," uncovering a boat and some farm equipment in the process.

The house, built in 1940, had been moved twice, and straight lines and even surfaces had long since disappeared. "Entertainment was rolling a marble across the floor," he remembers. "Frogs would visit you in the bathroom."

The couple lived with the discomfort for three years while they focused on improvements to the rest of the property. They put in a half-mile road and moved the barn site up to a hill, where they placed a forty-foot-by-ninety-foot pole barn especially designed for the goats.

Not far away they constructed a new home—a sand-colored frame house with a wraparound porch and lots of windows. Inside, the high-ceilinged great room is open to the kitchen and spacious enough for Linda's loom and several spinning wheels. From the upstairs hall, a balcony looks down to the first floor, and there are several bedrooms and an office, where Linda uses a computerized system to track the goats' bloodlines and fiber production.

The herd of goats now numbers sixty, though that fluctuates with the market and the amount of feed available. Hay is the biggest expense, Paul notes, reserved for feed in the winter months. The rest of the year, the goats browse in the pastures, which Linda and Paul watch carefully so the land is not outstripped. A pond provides habitat for ducks and geese. Every few years Paul and Linda also raise three or four turkeys for food.

Half a dozen Shetland sheep and five lambs—with more expected—share the barn with four cats, while three guard dogs (two Maremmas, and an Akbash) patrol for coyotes and cougars. There's also a Border Collie that helps keep the goats in order. "Goats are herdable," Paul says, "not well, but better than cats."

What started as a hobby quickly turned into a business. "We're oriented that way," Paul says. But a lot of what they needed to know they had to teach themselves.

Not long after they got their first cashmere goats, Linda and Paul bought *CashMirror*, a newsletter-magazine for owners and breeders. In those days there wasn't much information available, Paul remembers, and putting out the monthly publication, which they did for roughly eight years, allowed them to stay up-to-date and then share the information with others.

When it came to shearing, for example, neither Paul nor Linda had ever done it, but they felt they had to try. "We knew the first year we'd ruin the fleece, but we'd learn," he says. "We took pictures, wrote an article, and put it in the magazine. People thanked us!"

They also took a veterinary class at the local college extension to learn about keeping the animals healthy, as well as what to do during kidding season. "The first thing they do is give you an elbow-length rubber glove," Paul says darkly. "But goats are easy breeders with few problems. That's why we chose them."

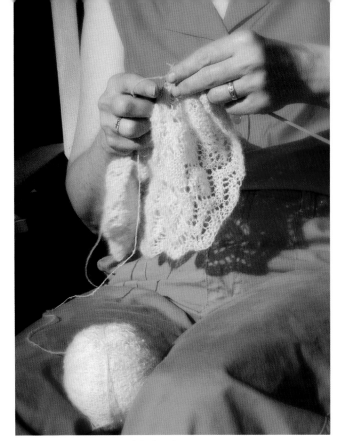

Lace takes shape in Linda's hands.

And although both Paul and Linda continue to hold down "day jobs," their knack for organization has led to routines that allow them to care for the animals efficiently. They're up by six thirty in the morning. Linda watches the news and enjoys coffee in bed before heading to her office. (She was appointed county treasurer when her predecessor retired in midterm, and she ran—and won—in 2004.)

Meanwhile, Paul lets out the dogs and checks on the animals. The sheep are confined in the barn at night; the goats usually come in at dark. They feed the animals once a day. "One person can do it in half an hour," Linda says, "which is important in case Paul is traveling."

If he's home, Paul might take time out to work on a fence. The perimeter enclosure is sectioned off so the goats can do weed control on smaller areas. "But you always like to have better fences," he says. "Some people play golf. Some fix fences."

And strong fences are needed to separate the male and the female goats. "The bucks are big, with big horns," he notes. "One little fence won't keep them from the does. I try to at least keep two fences and a road—and a fire hose—between them."

Periodically, often on weekends, the couple shares maintenance chores such as trimming hooves, worming, or vaccinating the animals. But several times a year there are the bigger projects: shearing, breeding, and kidding.

A large loom commands Linda's attention in the living room.

"The goats start growing cashmere at the end of June, and they're done in December," Linda says. You need to shear before they begin to shed the undercoat that constitutes the fine, valuable fiber. Happily, the couple's shearing skills have improved since their first efforts. Though Linda hand-combs out the cashmere on a few prized animals, the majority are shorn over a couple of weekends, usually in February. They send the fiber to be commercially "dehaired," which means separating the undercoat from the outercoat. Finally, the cashmere is processed into roving and some yarn.

As for breeding, Goat Knoll Farm tries to maintain a variety of colors in the herd, but the object is always more and better fiber. Linda and Paul strive for fineness, crimping (the waviness of a fiber strand), and good length. But these qualities don't all come together, Linda points out. "Some of those elements are contrary to each other. And as goats age, their fiber gets coarser, so you want them to start out with fine enough fiber so that when they're old, it's still considered cashmere."

"We have several blood lines," Paul says. They use Linda's database to check the genetics and the quality of fleece over generations. And though cashmere is their

primary focus, they also market the goats themselves. "Lately," he says, "we even offered 'starter kits,' which were two pregnant does."

The kids and lambs arrive in spring, a favorite time at Goat Knoll Farm. "I absolutely love it," says Paul. "The kids will be looking for a drink fifteen minutes after they're born. They're bouncing around in an hour. Next day the mothers have lost control."

The animal care keeps the couple active. "You don't have to think about what to do for exercise," says Linda, who is a trim five foot five. "The only question is are the goats keeping us young or making us old?"

Paul, who is six feet tall and 185 pounds, has a definite answer: "The goats have made me healthy," he asserts. "I had a heart attack at forty, but now they can't find any damage. I've given up most of my medications. In the past I belonged to health clubs. Now I'm on the goat diet."

The reward for all of Paul and Linda's efforts is fiber—and for a dyed-in-the-cashmere craftsperson like Linda, that's no small thing. "Cashmere spoils you for knitting," she says.

"It's softer and doesn't fuzz up like mohair." Linda has been knitting her entire life. "My grandmother taught me before I went to school."

Evenings, after work, are for crafts projects—and there are plenty to choose from. "After we bought the goats, I took up spinning," she says, "because I needed to know about fiber. My sister showed me. Now I spin all the time." Just a year ago, Linda started weaving. The huge loom— "the size of a grand piano"—sits in the living room, not far from two floor rugs Linda made using dyed yarn from her own sheep. "I love weaving," she says. "Now I'm into 'start-to-finish' things, pieces made from our own wool that we've sheared, washed, carded, spun, dyed, and woven."

For her next project, Linda has her eye on a pattern for a coat—a long hooded one with fringe on the side. "I'll have to spin the wool, then dye and weave it," she says. The finished fabric wouldn't need to be cut, merely seamed. "I want to finish it by the County Fair. Then I'd like to do more weaving with cashmere. There are always a zillion projects. Maybe lap robes," she says, thinking out loud.

The cashmere ranges in color from white, to several shades of brown, to gray. (Though some goats look black, there is no true black fiber.) The colors are luscious, but occasionally Linda will dye the yarn, just to experiment. "I've been playing with overdye," she says. "Instead of using white yarn, I used brown and dyed it red. It was beautiful— with more depth."

And there are always socks. "They're instant gratification," Linda says. "Cashmere . . . that's the ultimate sock!" She has acquired a circular sock-knitting machine that dates to around 1920. "It's hand-cranked, and I'd love to learn to use that."

Ever the businesswoman, Linda remembers a pair of cashmere socks she brought to a sheep association meeting. Everyone asked about buying them, so she finally named a price that accounted for the hours she'd spent knitting. "It was high," she remembers, too high to attract any takers. "But if you could knit a pair of cashmere socks in an evening, then it would be reasonable, and you could still make money."

Though Paul has tried his hand at weaving, most of the crafts fall to Linda. Other projects call for them to work together. In the past they've kept bees and produced honey flavored by the Willamette Valley's prolific wild black-berries. Recent harsh winters put an end to their last hive, but there are plans to start up beekeeping again.

Though most Goat Knoll animals are sheared, Linda demonstrates how to rake a kid's fiber (top) and the cashmere result (above).

Linda and Paul admire the fruits of their new greenhouse (above). Below: A mouthful of grass equals goat joy.

"Working with the bees is fun," Linda says. It's a way to clear one's mind of other projects. "When a thousand insects are trying to get into your suit, there's no time to think about work."

And last year was the first year they had a big garden. The soil in their area is normally poor, but they cleaned out the barn and "took the mix of straw and manure and used it in the garden. It was a jungle," says Linda, who likes to cook everything from scratch—from pancakes and stew to sauces and breads. "Peppers, broccoli, squash, corn, tomatoes . . . everything thrived." What Linda didn't use immediately, she froze or canned for the future.

The latest innovation on Goat Knoll Farm is a redwood-and-glass greenhouse, designed to start annuals and vegetables. "My goal is to produce salad vegetables all year," Linda says.

The greenhouse came "in a million parts" that the couple had to assemble. "Paul and I are still speaking. But we wonder if the thousand dollars we saved putting it together ourselves will pay for marriage counseling."

Still, there's the promise of all those good greens. "The stuff you grow yourself . . . there's no comparison," she says. "And the goats will eat the excess."

The Essence of Soft

The very word "cashmere" has become synonymous with luxury, conjuring up visions of the softest sweaters, the warmest scarves. For generations, cashmere goats were raised exclusively by nomadic herders in Mongolian deserts and Chinese mountains. Even now, 90 percent of the world's cashmere comes from those exotic corners of the world. Gradually, however, goat farms in Australia, New Zealand, and Scotland have joined the market, and about thirty years ago, animals were imported to the United States as well.

What may be surprising, though, is that there is no specific cashmere breed. All goats except Angoras produce cashmere, which is the animal's fine undercoat, protected by a coarser layer of guard hair. Cashmere goats are simply those bred commercially to enhance their fiber.

"To be called cashmere, the fiber must be less than 18.5 microns thick," Paul explains. That translates to .0007215 inch. Other factors, including crimp and length, are also important. To be marketable, the fibers must be at least one and a quarter inches long. "We aim for two inches," he says. And the fleece, which grows from June to December, must be removed every year, or the goat will naturally shed its winter coat and the valuable fiber will be lost.

In Asia, the cashmere is raked off the animals by hand. In the United States, breeders with only a few animals can comb out the fiber, which is more easily separated from the outercoat that way. Those with bigger herds usually shear the fleeces, which must then be sent to a dehairing mill.

A good cashmere doe produces about four ounces of fine fiber each year, notes Paul, which means it takes three goats to grow enough fleece for a sweater. Think about that the next time you snuggle into a cashmere turtleneck.

Goats on the knoll.

Luna Lace Scarf

Designer: Linda Fox

Named for the newest kid on the farm (shown with the model), this floaty, beautiful scarf only takes one skein of cashmere yarn, making it an affordable luxury. Don't be dismayed if it looks like nothing special while you're knitting it; lace really sings once it is blocked.

Skill Level
Intermediate

Size
One size

Finished Measurement
8" x 50" (20.5cm x 127cm)

Materials
 1 skein Goat Knoll, 100% cashmere, laceweight yarn, 275 yd (251.5m), 1 oz (28.5g), in any natural color

US size 8 (5mm) needles, or size needed to obtain gauge

Gauge
26½ stitches and 19 rows = 4" (10cm) in pattern stitch after blocking

Lace Scarf

Loosely cast on 55 stitches.

Row 1: K2, k2tog *k3, yo, k1, yo, k3, k3tog; repeat from * 4 times, ending k3, yo, k1, yo, k3, k2tog, k2.
Row 2: Knit across the row.

Repeat rows 1–2 until you are out of yarn, or until the desired scarf length has been obtained.

Finishing

Bind off loosely.

Block so as to open up the lace.

Warming a tiny kid in her embrace, a Goat Knoll visitor (opposite) wears two scarves in different colors. Above: spinning cashmere and the fiber's provenance (top).

Worf's Cashmere Socks

Designer: Linda Fox

A basic stockinette sock is transformed when striped in two natural shades of cashmere. These are named for the granddaddy of the Goat Knoll bucks, a goat with personality to spare. Cashmere yarn is not a very durable yarn for socks. To lengthen the life of your socks, you may want to consider using a sock reinforcing yarn in the heel and toe. The two skeins required for this pattern should give you just enough for two pair of medium women's socks, with the main color and contrast color reversed on the second pair.

Skill Level
Intermediate

Size
Women's 7–8

Finished Measurements
Leg length: 6½" (16.5cm)
Foot length: 9" (23cm)
Circumference at ball of foot: 8" (20.5 cm)

Materials
Goat Knoll, 100% cashmere, 3-ply yarn, 250 yd (228.5), 2 oz (56.5g): 1 skein in oatmeal, main color (MC), and 1 skein in dark brown, contrast color (CC)

US size 2 (2.75mm) set of 4 double-pointed needles, or size needed to obtain gauge (wooden recommended). Tapestry needle

Gauge
32 stitches and 48 rows = 4" (10cm) in stockinette stitch

Socks

Using MC, loosely cast on 60 stitches—20 stitches on each of 3 needles. Join, being careful not to twist the initial row.
Work k1, p1 ribbing in the round for 1¾" (4.5cm).
Change to CC and knit 10 rounds.
Change to MC and knit 5 rounds.
Continue working in 5-round stripes, alternating colors until you finish the fourth stripe in MC.

Heel Flap

Place 30 stitches of MC on a needle for the heel flap and place 15 stitches on each of the other 2 needles for the instep.
Change to CC and work on heel flap stitches only.
Row 1 (RS): *Slip 1, k1; repeat from * to end.
Row 2(WS): Slip 1, purl to end.
Repeat rows 1–2 until the heel flap measures 2¼" (5.5cm), ending with a right-side row.

Turn Heel

Row 1: Slip 1, p15, p2tog, p1, turn.
Row 2: Slip 1, k3, slip 1, k1, pass the slipped stitch over, k1, turn.
Row 3: Slip 1, purl to 1 stitch before the last turning and then p2tog, p1, turn.

Row 4: Slip 1, knit to 1 stitch before the last turning and then slip 1, k1, pass a slipped stitch over, k1, turn.
Repeat rows 3 and 4 until there are 16 stitches left, ending on a right-side row.

On the right side, pick up and knit 16 stitches along the edge of the heel flap. Place these stitches and half of the heel stitches on a needle (needle 1).
Knit across the 30 instep stitches. Place the stitches on a needle (needle 2).
Pick up and knit 16 stitches along the other side of the heel flap, then knit half of the heel stitches onto the same needle (needle 3).

Knit one complete round on needles 1, 2, and 3. (The beginning of the round is in the middle of the heel stitches.)

Shape Gusset
Round 1: On needle 1, knit to the last 3 stitches, then k2tog, k1. On needle 2, knit across the instep stitches. On needle 3, k1, slip 1, k1, pass the slipped stitch over, knit to the end.
Round 2: Knit 1 round with no decreases.

Repeat rounds 1 and 2 of gusset shaping, changing yarn colors every 5 rounds as before—60 stitches total: 15 stitches each on needles 1 and 3 and 30 stitches on needle 2.

Continue to knit rounds in the striped pattern until you have 6 rows of the first color after the heel or until you reach about 2" (5cm) from the desired sock length.

Shape Toe
Change to MC.
Round 1: On needle 1, knit to the last 3 stitches, k2tog, k1. On needle 2, k1, slip 1, k1, pass the slipped stitch over, and knit to the last 3 stitches, k2tog, k1.
On needle 3, k1, slip 1, k1, pass the slipped stitch over, knit to the end.
Round 2: Knit 1 round with no decreases.
Repeat rounds 1 and 2 until 20 stitches remain.

Divide stitches onto 2 needles for top and bottom of toe, and cut the yarn, leaving an 8" (20.5cm) tail. Using a tapestry needle, kitchener stitch the toe closed. Weave in end.

Old Mill Farm
Building on a Network of Family and Community

Mendocino, California

Playful exuberance describes Barbara Sochacki's McNab Collies (opposite) as well as her farmhouse. Above (clockwise from top left): freshly gathered eggs, a sheep in lush grass, Old Mill Farm yarn, salad greens.

The road to Old Mill Farm begins in Mendocino, a stunning corner of the California coast, then continues inland and upward and finally turns into a dirt track that curves through towering redwoods and Douglas firs. On a chilly, clear morning, shafts of golden sunlight beam through the forest, as breathtakingly beautiful as rays of light through a stained-glass church window.

It was the redwoods that first attracted settlers to the area in the 1850s. As the lumber industry here boomed, the newcomers put up the New England–style cottages that give Mendocino its distinctive look and turned the town into a busy port where logs were loaded onto schooners waiting offshore. Among the homesteaders arriving around the turn of the century was a Finnish family named Thompson, who built a house at the top of a ridge, between Berry Gulch and the Little North Fork of the Big River. There they cut trees and fashioned ties for the logging railways that shuttled timber to the coast. The remains of the old mill, which gave their property its name, are still evident, but today the land is part of an organic, sustainable farm that raises a bounty of healthful produce. It also is home to Barbara, Ben, and Cas Sochacki, garden manager Colin Fissenden, a bevy of interns and apprentices, three McNab Collies, barn cats, myriad pigs, and two dozen sheep.

The natural brown, gray, and white wool and yarn that comes from Old Mill Farm is organic, too, the result of the efforts of several generations of two intertwined families.

But fiber is only part of the Old Mill Farm story, which has a lot to do with the idealism of the 1960s, family ties, and the hand of fate.

The Thompsons, who raised a dozen children, never quite found time to finish constructing their house. They eventually sold the property to one of their sons, who, in turn, sold it to a lumber company that harvested valuable redwoods off the land for several decades. By the early 1970s, that firm, too, was ready to sell.

Meanwhile, in the 1950s, artists had discovered Mendocino, which had declined from its earlier heyday, and a decade later the area's beauty and remoteness began to attract hippies and others seeking an alternative lifestyle. One of those was Chuck Hinsch. Old Mill Farm was just what he was looking for.

"Chuck wanted to go back to the land," remembers Barbara, who married Hinsch in 1970. "Though he had never farmed, he had good ideas. He was a real idealist." The couple came west together from Kentucky in 1969 on a quest that took them first to the Family of the Mystic Arts Commune in Oregon (which attained fifteen minutes of fame as part of a *Life* cover story in July of that year). "I didn't have the right shoes," for the hippie lifestyle, remembers Barbara, whose wardrobe in those days ran to Papagallo flats and Lilly Pulitzer dresses.

On a winter morning, though, the lively, sociable, fifty-eight-year-old is wearing jeans and a blue turtleneck sweater accented by a thick velour scarf as she makes tea

Barbara and her husband, Ben, savor coffee (opposite) on a California morning. Below: Cas Sochacki uses a bucket of feed to run the flock between two pastures.

Knee deep in lunch, Old Mill Farm sheep find plenty to graze on.

in the farmhouse kitchen and continues the tale of how she and Chuck came to Mendocino.

After the summer of 1969, the couple moved to Haight-Ashbury and then to Mill Valley, where their son, Anderson, was born in 1972. Chuck bought Old Mill Farm—320 wooded acres, surrounded by public forestlands—a year later. Their nearest neighbor, about a mile away, was the Mendocino Woodlands Group Camp, where schoolchildren and members of other organizations often spend summer sojourns. The Hinsches lived in the barn at first, then in a tepee, and finally they moved into the old Thompson house, which was still unfinished and had no indoor plumbing.

But Chuck began to put his environmental ideas into practice, experimenting with solar power, raising dairy goats, and growing vegetables. "His mission for Old Mill Farm was to educate and share with the community," says Barbara, adding that he would work with boys' and girls' clubs, taking the kids on wagon rides and teaching them to make goat's milk cheese. Chuck also began to raise Merino and Jacob sheep. And he sent the fleeces to a wool cooperative near Sacramento to be scoured, carded, and spun into yarn.

It was a rugged life for a young woman with a baby. In 1975 the couple divorced, and Barbara moved back to Mill Valley, where she met and married Ben Sochacki, a general contractor. She returned to Mendocino with Ben soon after, so Anderson could attend school in the town. It was there that their son, Cas, was born in 1979. Ben, Barbara, and the two boys moved to Kentucky two years later, but the ties to Mendocino had been forged.

As Anderson followed his own career path, his half-brother, Cas, was drawn to the Old Mill Farm lifestyle. At twenty-seven, Cas stands more than six feet tall, sports a black handlebar mustache and goatee, wears plaid flannel shirts and jeans, and looks utterly at home in the California hills. "Chuck was a big part of my character development and personality," he says, remembering his first discussion about working at the farm when he was in fifth grade and visiting Mendocino. "I came out and spent time with Chuck a few times in high school, too."

Fascinated by forestry and geology at college in Tennessee, Cas enrolled in a natural resources program. "Geology gives you a different eye when you're looking at the earth," he says, and that ultimately pertains to soils, no small thing for someone who wanted to live on the land.

He spent a junior semester in New Zealand and planned to return to Mendocino to work at Old Mill Farm both before his senior year and after college. But, in 2000, Chuck Hinsch died in a tractor accident.

Anderson inherited the farm, and though he pursued his own business interests, it was important for him to carry on what his father had lived his life for. That was a sentiment Cas shared. "When Chuck died, I decided I wanted to make everything work somehow," he says, as did his parents. The entire family pitched in to keep the farm operating.

Barbara and Ben returned from Kentucky, "where we had a real life and real jobs," she says. And after he graduated, Cas took over the management of Old Mill Farm. Half a dozen years later, the traditions begun by Chuck survive with sales of organic meat, produce, and yarn at farmers' markets and to businesses around Mendocino. The farm also environmentally harvests timber. And Cas and his family work hard to build on the original vision of sustainability and education. You can't feed the world with a farm like this, Cas notes, but you can start by feeding your community.

The Thompson house remains at the heart of Old Mill Farm. Its basic wooden rectangle has been painted yellow. There's now a second story with two bedrooms, as well as a bridge that leads to a wooden Mendocino-style water tower, which has been fitted with a sleeping loft, bath, and shower, and embellished—by a creative carpenter—with bay windows and skylights, decorative trim, and solar panels. "It's wood butcher architecture," Barbara says of the hippie-style carpentry.

The furnishings within are equally eclectic: Oriental carpets cover the wide plank floors. Leather couches and chairs face the stone fireplace and the TV. In another corner, sheep's fleeces soften the hard seats of directors' and barber chairs. Numerous stained glass panels refract the sunlight through the windows. "Chuck and I got them from Victorian houses they were tearing down in Louisville in the 1970s," says Barbara, "and brought them out here."

A poker slot machine, similarly salvaged from an old gambling den near Cincinnati, has a place in front of an upright piano. A second piano stands against another wall, flanked by a drum set and several guitars and amplifiers. (The instruments are evidence of another of Cas's passions—performing with his girlfriend's musical group, the Blushin' Roulettes.)

In the dining area, a telescope and a stack of mushroom guidebooks lie on a window seat, where a dried mesquite branch is hung with tiny lights and several miniature, felted sheep. A huge propane gas stove warms the kitchen, whose window faces a pasture, "where I can watch the ewes and lambs," says Barbara.

In addition to the main residence, Cas has his own house next door, built in a passive-solar design in the late 1970s from the wood of a single redwood tree. There are also cabins for the garden manager, interns, and apprentices, and one that visitors can rent, as well as redwood barns, storage sheds, pens, and chicken coops filled with equipment, animals, and notably, the makings of home-brewed beer. Everything—lights, computers, TV, and stereo—is solar-powered, with a propane generator as backup.

Nearing completion on the far side of the sheep pasture is a straw-bale house, constructed with the help of a nearby commune ("They call them intentional communities now,"

Cas delivers organic wares to Nicholas Petti (below, in hat) chef-owner of the Mendo Bistro. Chicken coop inspiration (right).

A knitting group at the Mendocino Yarn Shop.

notes Barbara) that specializes in natural building. Inside, tree trunk pillars reach to the open, beamed ceiling, clerestory windows bring in light, and natural plaster walls surround a powdered adobe floor. "We're building it as a community kitchen for some of the groups that camp or meet here," Barbara explains. The farm's calendar is filled with events like the annual sustainable living festival in the fall, visits by elementary schoolchildren, and an "alternative education week" for local high school students in the spring. A local spinner has also held several fiber festivals for spinners and weavers on the grounds.

Barbara points to some tufts of wool and a length of nubbly brown yarn curled in a bowl on a side table in the living room. "One of the kids probably made that with a drop spindle," she says, smiling.

Though Chuck Hinsch had his own sheep at Old Mill Farm years ago, those animals were gone by the time Cas came to run the place. The Sochackis began to replenish the flock in 2002, less for fiber than for their importance to the farm as a whole.

"We started with a Suffolk ewe called Mama," Cas remembers, "then got a black Suffolk ram, and picked up a couple of ewes from a winery up the coast." The breed was

versatile and good for meat, and they ate a lot of grass, which eliminated the need for mowing pastures. And though obtaining good fleece wasn't his initial goal, "sheep grow wool," Cas says, and on a sustainable farm you try to make the most of whatever resources you have. So wool became another of their products.

Later, word got around that they had pasture for sheep, and some weavers and spinners in neighboring Fort Bragg asked Cas to take some Cheviot-Karakul crosses.

The Suffolk ram is gone now, too. In his place there's a purebred Cheviot named Freddie Mac. "Cheviots are hardy," Cas says, as you'd expect from a breed that hails from the hills on the border between Scotland and England. And his flock has grown to roughly twenty-five. Cas keeps them on a schedule that fits the California climate and the needs of the farm.

He breeds the ewes in July, and they lamb around New Years. "They do just fine" in winter, Cas says, though he pastures them near the lambing pen, so he can "keep an eye on them." By the time spring rolls around, however, it's up to Colin, the garden manager, to move the animals from one place to another.

Colin, a slight, soft-spoken twenty-seven-year-old with a reddish beard and blond hair, came to Old Mill Farm in early 2006 after graduating from the agricultural program at Evergreen College in Washington State. "We'll make tiny pastures around the garden," he says in his deliberate way, "where the sheep can graze for a day or two. We move them around for mowing."

The sheep might stay in the bigger upper pasture for a week. "We get a few grazings out of a pasture, then in summertime, when the grass stops growing, we'll make a large pasture and feed them organically grown hay."

"They're sheared in June," Colin adds, by a shearer who comes to the farm every year, like an itinerant preacher visiting his flock. Old Mill still sends the wool clip to the same cooperative Chuck Hinsch used, and the resulting yarn is part of the offerings at weekly farmers' markets, from May through October. It's also on the shelves at the local yarn shop, where the town's knitters gather and socialize.

The sheep are about to be part of another Old Mill Farm project, too. A couple of years ago, Cas planted an acre of pinot noir grapes. But since there's a lot of manual labor involved in keeping the vines weed-free, and the Karakul-Cheviot sheep were short, "I got the idea of breeding them for the vineyard," Cas says. He plans to develop smaller and smaller animals. By the time the grapes are producing wine, he may actually have compact sheep able to graze beneath the vines without affecting the fruit.

Along with the sheep, Old Mill Farm raises pigs and is known for its organic pork, bacon, and sausage. But the greatest part of Colin's efforts is directed toward Old Mill Farm's extensive organic gardens and to supervising the interns who help him cultivate and harvest a variety of seasonal crops. His passion for the work is obvious. His parents weren't gardeners, he says, but "early on I was a nature nerd, and I stayed that way."

So during a Mendocino winter, while the new lambs are finding their way around the pasture, Colin is growing neat, tidy rows of lettuce, arugula, and frisée that run the length of a plastic-covered greenhouse. Outside he bends to show off a variety of brilliantly colored chard with orange veins and a chocolate leaf. "It's just gorgeous," he says.

Colin works closely with Cas to plant the crops that will sell well in farmers' markets and also meet the needs of their restaurant customers. "In the spring, we're the king of peas, and green beans through the summer." Warm weather brings abundant tomatoes, peppers, and eggplants.

And when he's asked about what he'd *like* to grow, Colin describes a cornucopia of vegetables—a greenhouse full of salad, plus melons, potatoes, onions, garlic, barley, hops, collards, cauliflower, broccoli, and of course, peas. He envisions produce to feed the farm and the community, cover crops to replenish the soil's nutrients and feed the animals, and something decorative. Inspired by the cut flowers he grew in college, Colin says he's "going to get big into flowers—snapdragons, zinnias, and sunflowers."

Meanwhile, there is compost to make, fruit trees and vines—pears, apples, plums, quince, berries—to manage, and honey to harvest in the fall. It all takes planning and coordination and the work of many people, from the permanent staff to a changing cast of interns and apprentices, who act as a field crew, beginning in the spring. There's a nonindustrial timber management plan in place, and the farm works with a forester and a logging company

Garden manager Colin Fissenden works in the greenhouse.

to sustainably harvest selected trees. And while Ben Sochacki has kept his outside contracting business, his carpentry and other handiwork is evident in the decks, cabinetry, and other additions to buildings all over the farm.

Intern Beverly Healy came from Cedar Rapids, Iowa, to see what organic farm life might be like. Blond and delicate-boned, she lives on the property in a large cabin heated by a woodstove and is happy to describe her routine to a visitor.

Monday morning begins with the weekly staff meeting. "Barbara cooks a really good breakfast," she notes, while the group sets out its priorities. There are always the sheep, pigs, and chickens to feed. Twice a week—once in winter—she helps pick, weigh, and clean vegetables; sometimes she runs the produce to restaurants in town. "We'll pick up used produce boxes and get table scraps" at the same time, she adds, to feed the pigs. "Our pigs eat really well."

If the farm work would be recognizable anywhere in the country, there are a few aspects of Old Mill Farm that bind it indelibly to this part of California. The three playful McNab Collies represent a variant of short-haired Scottish Border Collies developed by Alexander McNab in this very county more than a century ago. The quick, agile breed is renowned for intelligence, attention, and loyalty.

And there's one other unusual feature. In a clearing near the straw-bale house stands a labyrinth whose curving path is defined by a raised earth berm. Constructed in 2003 by earthwork artist Alex Champion, it invites a visitor to take a contemplative stroll. It's designed in a three-circuit Chartres pattern, Barbara says, adding, "For a year I held a full-moon walk in it." Groups of friends would come to follow the moonlit circuit.

The labyrinth seems an appropriate addition to an organic farm that began with a vision of going back to the land. For what could be more symbolic of finding one's center and physically connecting to the earth?

Redwoods Earflap Hat

Designer: Ann Hovey

On the northern California coast, free thinkers with personal style live where the redwoods meet the Pacific. A natural, handspun, wooly earflap hat, with daisy stitches around the edge, is just right for a chilly morning, after surfing, or on the beach watching the sea lions. Although you need two skeins of Old Mill Farm's yarn to make one hat, if you reverse the main color and contrast color, you'll have enough yarn to make a second one.

Skill Level
Intermediate

Sizes
Child (Adult)

Finished Measurements
Circumference: 18 (21)" (45.5 [53.5]cm)

Materials
Old Mill Farms, 100% wool, handspun yarn, 200 yd (183m), 3½ oz (99g): 1 skein in Natural Dark Brown, main color (MC), and 1 skein in Natural Light Gray, contrast color (CC)

US size 8 (5mm), 16" (40cm) long circular needle, or size needed to obtain gauge
US size 8 (5mm) set of double-pointed needles
Tapestry needle

Gauge
16 stitches and 24 rows = 4" (10cm) in stockinette stitch

Earflap (Make 2)

With MC and circular needle, cast on 2 stitches. Turn.
Knit in front and back of both stitches—4 stitches. Turn.
Knit in front and back of the first stitch, k2, knit in front and back of the last stitch—6 stitches. Turn.

Continue increasing in the first and last stitch and knitting stitches in between on every row (garter stitch), until there are 12 (14) stitches. Turn.

Work daisy chain stitch over the next 2 rows as follows: with CC, purl 4 (5); over the next 4 stitches, purl, but wrap yarn twice around the right-hand needle for each stitch, then purl the remaining 4 (5) stitches. Turn.

Purl 4 (5), slip the next 4 stitches onto the right-hand needle, dropping extra wraps as they are slipped. Pass all 4 stitches back onto the left-hand needle and work k1, p1, k1, p1 into all 4 stitches at once (*this operation should be done somewhat loosely!*), then purl 4 (5). Break off yarn. Turn.

With MC, purl 1 row, turn.

Knit the next 8 (10) rows. Break off yarn and push the earflap to the end of the needle.

Make a second earflap in the same manner, but do not cut the yarn. Turn.

Join for Hat
With the right side of the earflaps facing, knit across the 12 (14) stitches of the first earflap, then cast on 30 (34) stitches; knit across the 12 (14) stitches of the second earflap, then cast on 18 (22) stitches—72 (84) stitches total.

Join stitches carefully into a round to begin the hat.

Rows 1–3: *K4, p2; repeat from * around.
Work 2 rows daisy chain ribbing:
Row 4: Leaving MC inside the hat and with CC, *knit the next 4 stitches, wrapping yarn twice around the right-hand needle for each stitch, k2; repeat from * around.
Row 5: *Slip the next 4 stitches onto the right-hand needle, dropping extra wraps as they are slipped, pass all 4 stitches back onto the left-hand needle and (loosely) work k1, p1, k1, p1, into all four stitches at the same time, p2; repeat from * around—12 (14) daisy stitches made. Break off CC.
With MC, knit 1 row, then repeat rows 1–3.
Row 9: Begin working even in stockinette stitch until the hat measures 4 (4½)" (10 [11.5]cm).

Shape Crown
When the hat becomes too narrow for the circular needle, switch to double-pointed needles.
Row 1: *K10, k2tog; repeat from * 6 (7) times around—66 (77) stitches.
Row 2: Work even.
Repeat rows 1–2, always having 1 stitch less between decreases on decrease rows until 36 (35) stitches remain. Work row 1 only (k2tog around) until 12 (14) stitches remain.

Work 2 rows even.

Next row: K2tog around—6 (7) stitches remain.
Move all 6 (7) stitches onto one double-pointed needle and work 2 rows of I-cord as follows:

Knit across to end; push stitches back to the other end of the needle, pulling yarn snugly behind the stitches, and knit across all stitches. Repeat for 5" (12.5cm) or the desired length of the I-cord.

Now work *k1, k2tog; repeat from * once, k0 (1)—4 (5) stitches remain. Continue working I-cord for about 2" (5cm). K2tog twice, k0 (1), turn, slip 1, k1 (k2tog for the larger size), pass the slipped stitch over, fasten off. Cut yarn, leaving about 7" (18cm) tail.

Earflap Dangles

With right side facing, dark brown yarn, and a double-pointed needle, pick up and knit 2 stitches in the first two stitches of the earflap. Turn. Purl twice in each stitch. Turn. Work I-cord for 4½" (11.5cm). Cut the yarn, leaving a 7" (18cm) tail. Repeat for the second earflap.

Finishing

Make 3 tassels or pom-poms and attach one to each I-cord. Weave in ends.

Mendocino Vest

Designer: Ann Hovey

This artfully cabled vest with an eyelet scalloped edge is perfect for those chilly mornings.

Skill Level
Intermediate

Size
One Size

Finished Measurements
Chest: 37½" (95.5cm)
Length: 22" (56cm)

Materials
 3 skeins Old Mill Farm, 100% wool, mill-spun yarn, 200 yd (183m), 3½ oz (99g), in medium gray

US size 8 needles (5mm), or size needed to obtain gauge
US size 7 (4.5mm), 16" (40cm) long circular needle
US size 7 (4.5mm) double-pointed needles
Stitch holders
Stitch markers
Tapestry needle
7 buttons, 5/8" (15mm) in diameter

Gauge
16 stitches and 24 rows = 4" (10cm) in stockinette stitch using size 8 needles

Back
With larger needles and the long-tail method, cast on 75 stitches.

Eyelet Edge
Row 1 (RS): K1, *yo, k2tog; repeat from * to the end of the row.
Row 2: Knit.

Work rows 1–8 of the chart once as indicated; repeat rows 9–12 until the Back measures 12" (30.5cm), ending with a wrong-side row.

Shape Armholes
At the beginning of the next 2 rows, work across the first 5 stitches in pattern and place them on stitch holders.
Bind off 3 stitches at the beginning of the next 2 rows.
Bind off 2 stitches at the beginning of the next 2 rows.
Bind off 1 stitch at the beginning of the next 2 rows.
Continue in pattern for remaining 53 stitches as established until the piece measures 20" (51cm), ending with the right side facing for the next row.

Back Neck Shaping
With right side facing, work across the first 22 stitches in pattern, and place the next 9 stitches on a stitch holder for the back neck. Turn.

Right Shoulder
At neck edge, bind off 3 stitches. Work across in pattern.
Work 1 row even.
At the beginning of the next 2 wrong-side rows, bind off 2 stitches. Continue to work in pattern on the remaining 15 stitches until the Back measures 22" (56cm). Place the shoulder stitches on a stitch holder and cut the yarn.

Left Shoulder
Rejoin the yarn to remaining stitches. At neck edge, bind off 3 stitches. Work across in pattern. Work 1 row even.
At the beginning of the next 2 right side rows, bind off 2 stitches. Continue to work in pattern on the remaining 15 stitches until the Back measures 22" (56cm). Place the shoulder stitches on a stitch holder and cut the yarn.

Mendocino Vest Key

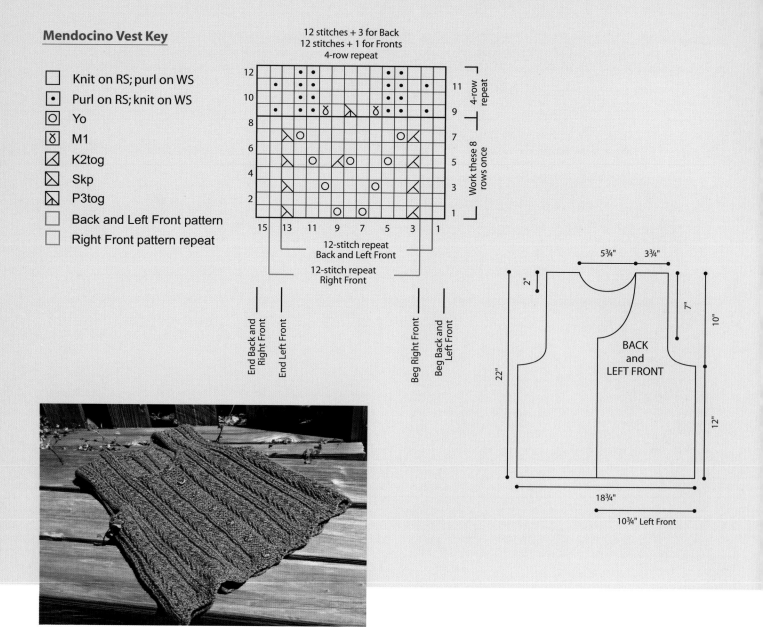

☐	Knit on RS; purl on WS
☐	Purl on RS; knit on WS
Ⓞ	Yo
☒	M1
☒	K2tog
☒	Skp
☒	P3tog
☐	Back and Left Front pattern
☐	Right Front pattern repeat

12 stitches + 3 for Back
12 stitches + 1 for Fronts
4-row repeat

4-row repeat

Work these 8 rows once

12-stitch repeat
Back and Left Front

12-stitch repeat
Right Front

End Back and Right Front
End Left Front
Beg Right Front
Beg Back and Left Front

5¾" 3¾"
2"
7"
10"
22"
12"

BACK
and
LEFT FRONT

18¾"
10¾" Left Front

Left Front

With larger needles cast on 43 stitches.

Row 1: *K2tog, yo; repeat from * to the last 7 stitches, k1, place marker, k6.

Row 2: Knit. Eyelet edge is now completed.

Next row: Keeping the last 6 stitches in garter stitch for the button band as established, work rows 1–8 of the chart once, beginning and ending and working the pattern repeat as indicated on the chart. Keeping the last 6 stitches in garter stitch as established, work rows 9–12 until the piece measures the same to the armhole shaping as the Back, ending with a wrong-side row.

Shape Armhole

Knit 5 stitches and slip them onto a stitch holder. Work across the row in pattern.

At the beginning of the next right-side row, bind off 3 stitches. Work across the row in pattern.

At the beginning of the next right-side row, bind off 2 stitches. Work across the row in pattern.

At the beginning of the next right-side row, bind off 1 stitch. Work across the row in pattern.

Continue to work in pattern as established on 32 stitches until the piece measures 15" (38cm), ending with a right-side row.

Shape Front Neck

Work across the first 9 stitches in pattern and slip them onto a stitch holder. Continue across the row in pattern.
At the neck edge, bind off 3 stitches. Work across in pattern.
Bind off 2 stitches at the neck edge twice.
Bind off 1 stitch at the neck edge once.

Continue to work the remaining 15 stitches in pattern for the shoulder until the piece measures 22" (56cm).
Place all stitches on a stitch holder and cut the yarn.

Right Front

With larger needles, cast on 43 stitches.
Row 1: K6, place marker, k1, *yo, k2tog; repeat from * to the end of the row.
Row 2: Knit. Eyelet edge is now completed.
Next row: Keeping the first 6 stitches in garter stitch for the buttonhole band as established, work rows 1–8 of the chart once, working the first buttonhole on the first row as given below and working the pattern repeat as indicated on the chart.
Work 6 buttonholes evenly spaced as follows: On the first row of the chart and every following fourteenth row, work buttonhole—k3, yo, k2tog, k1, work in pattern across row.

Keeping the first 6 stitches in garter stitch as established, work rows 9–12 of the chart until the piece measures the same to the armhole shaping as the Back, ending with a right-side row.

Shape Armhole

Work 5 stitches and slip them onto a stitch holder. Work across the row in pattern.
At the beginning of the next wrong-side row, bind off 3 stitches. Work across the row in pattern.
At the beginning of the next wrong-side row, bind off 2 stitches. Work across the row in pattern.
At the beginning of the next wrong-side row, bind off 1 stitch. Work across the row in pattern.
Continue to work in pattern as established on 32 stitches until the piece measures 15" (38 cm), ending with a wrong-side row.

Shape Front Neck

Work across the first 9 stitches in pattern and slip them onto a stitch holder. Continue across the row in pattern. Work one row straight.
At the beginning of the next row, bind off 3 stitches. Work across in pattern.
Bind off 2 stitches at the neck edge twice more.
Bind off 1 stitch at the neck edge once.

Continue to work the remaining 15 stitches in pattern for the shoulder until the piece measures 22" (56cm).
Place all stitches on a stitch holder and cut the yarn.

Finishing

Neck

Join the front and back shoulders together using a three-needle bind-off:
Place each set of shoulder stitches on a double-pointed needle. Turn the vest inside out, right sides together. Hold the right front shoulder needle and the right back shoulder needle together in your left hand. Insert a third double-pointed needle through the first stitch on both needles, knit. Repeat with the next stitch on each needle and then pass the first stitch over the second stitch as for a bind-off. Continue in this manner until the end. Break the yarn and pass through the last stitch. Repeat for the other shoulder seam.

With the circular needle and right side facing, knit across 9 stitches on the Right Front, pick up and knit 30 stitches along Right Front edge to the shoulder seam, pick up and knit 23 stitches along the back neck (including the 9 left on the holder), pick up and knit 30 stitches along the Left Front neck and then knit 9 stitches from Left Front stitch holder—101 stitches total.
Knit 1 row. Turn.
K3, make a buttonhole, k1, *yo, k2tog; repeat from * to the last 7 stitches, k7.
Knit 1 row. Turn.
Bind off in knit.

Sew side seams.

Armholes

With the circular needle and right side facing, knit 5 stitches from the first stitch holder, then pick up and knit 64 stitches evenly spaced around the armhole, then knit 5 stitches from the second stitch holder—74 stitches.
Join into a round and purl 1 row.
On next row work (yo, k2tog) around.
Purl 1 row.
On the next row, bind off in knit.

Sew buttons on the Left Front button band to correspond to the buttonholes.

Using the tapestry needle, weave in all ends.

Block carefully.

Abbreviations

"	inch(es)		oz	ounce(s)
* *	repeat instructions between the asterisks as directed		p or P	purl
			p2tog	purl 2 stitches together
*	repeat instructions following the single asterisk as directed		p3tog	purl 3 stitches together
			p2sso	pass 2 slipped stitch over
CC	contrasting color		RS	right side
cm	centimeter(s)		skp	slip, knit, pass stitch over—one stitch decreased
g	gram		sl	slip
k or K	knit		sl1p	slip 1 purlwise
k2tog	knit 2 stitches together		ssk	slip, slip, knit these 2 stitches together—a decrease
m	meter(s)		tbl	through back loop
M1	make 1 stitch—lifted increase		WS	wrong side
MC	main color		yd	yard(s)
mm	millimeter(s)		yo	yarn over

Shear Spirit Fiber and Material Sources

With the exception of Old Mill Farm, all of the yarns used with Shear Spirit patterns may be obtained directly from the farm or ranch. We have also listed retail stores and shows and festivals where farmers and ranchers exhibit their fiber products. Some farms have only one source. If you wish to visit any of the farms or ranches, please call or e-mail ahead of time.

Meadowcroft Farm

Seacolors Yarn
Nanney Kennedy
45 Hopkins Road, Washington, Maine 04574
207-845-2587
queen@getwool.com, www.getwool.com

Shows & Festivals:
- Common Ground Fair, Unity, Maine
- New York State Sheep & Wool Festival, Dutchess County Fairgrounds, Rhinebeck, New York
- Maryland Sheep & Wool Festival, Howard County Fairgrounds, Frederick, Maryland
- Stitches East

Buttons: Sea glass buttons are available through Meadowcroft Farm and from Island Sea Glass Company, 52 Brighton Hill Road, Hebron, Maine 04238, 207-966-2937, islandseaglass@aol.com

Tregellys Fiber Farm

Jody and Ed Cothey
15 Dodge Branch Road, Hawley, Massachusetts 01339
413-625-6448
tregellys@hotmail.com, www.tregellysfibers.com

Tregellys's fiber is sold exclusively through Botanical Shades.
Jody McKenzie
1084 Main Street, Waldoboro, Maine 04572
207-832-4303
jodymckenzie@adelphia.net, www.botanicalshades.com

Shows & Festivals:
- Fiber Twist Marketplace and Open Farm Tour, Deerfield, Massachusetts
- Maine Fiber Frolic, Windsor, Maine
- Maryland Sheep & Wool Festival, Howard County Fairgrounds, Frederick, Maryland
- Massachusetts Sheep & Wool Festival, Cummington, Massachusetts
- New York State Sheep & Wool Festival, Dutchess County Fairgrounds, Rhinebeck, New York

Autumn House Farm

Ken and Harriet Knox
1001 Locust Road, Rochester Mills, Pennsylvania 15771
724-286-9596
vdicken@penn.com, www.autumnhousefarm.com

Buttons: The buttons on the Cassandra Cardigan must be ordered directly through Autumn House Farm.

Retail Sources:

Rosie's Yarn Cellar
2017 Locust Street, Philadelphia, Pennsylvania 19103
215-977-9276
rosie@rosiesyarncellar.com, www.rosiesyarncellar.com

Stix-n-Stitches
211 Glenridge Avenue, Montclair, New Jersey 07042
973-796-2860, www.stixnstitches.com

Knit One
2721 Murray Avenue, Pittsburgh, Pennsylvania 15217
412-421-6666
stacey@knitone.biz, www.knitone.biz

Shows & Festivals:
- Maryland Sheep & Wool Festival, Howard County Fairgrounds, Frederick, Maryland
- Michigan Fiber Festival, Allegan, Michigan
- New York Sheep & Wool Festival, Dutchess County Fairgrounds, Rhinebeck, New York

Misty Meadow Icelandics Farm

Judy and Tom McDowell
6725 West Branch Road, Minnetrista, Minnesota 55364
952-472-0883
judy@mistymeadowicelandics.com
www.mistymeadowicelandics.com

Shows & Festivals:
- Shepherd's Harvest, Washington County Fairgrounds, Lake Elmo, Minnesota

Kai Ranch

Lisa Shell
Route 1, PO Box 293-C, Lexington, Texas 78947
512-273-2709
kai1mohair@yahoo.com, www.kairanch.com

Shows & Festivals:
- Armadillo Christmas Bazaar, Austin, Texas
- Estes Park Wool Market, Stanley Park Fairgrounds, Estes Park, Colorado
- Taos Wool Festival, Kit Carson Park, Taos, New Mexico

Victory Ranch

Ken and Carol Weisner
Darcy Weisner, Manager
PO Box 680, Mora, New Mexico 87732
505-387-2254
info@victoryranch.com, www.victoryranch.com

The Ranch has a large retail store that carries luxury clothing and yarn on the premises.

Lazy J Diamond Ranch

Jay Begay Jr.
PO Box 1232, Tuba City, Arizona 86045
928-606-8250
jay_bjr@yahoo.com
www.geocities.com/jay_bjr/LazyJDiamondRanch

Shows & Festivals:
- Fiberfest EUREKA, Eureka, Montana
- Maryland Sheep and Wool Festival, Howard County Fairgrounds, Frederick, Maryland
- Sheep Is Life Celebration, Tsaile, Arizona
- Taos Wool Festival, Kit Carson Park, Taos, New Mexico

Thirteen Mile Farm

Becky Weed and Dave Tyler
13000 Springhill Road, Belgrade, Montana 59714
406-388-4945
becky@lambandwool.com or www.lambandwool.com

Retail Sources:
Please see Thirteen Mile Farm's website for more locations.

Amazing Yarns
2559 Woodland Place, Emerald Hills, California 94062
650-306-9218
amazing5@ix.netcom.com, www.amazingyarn.com

Stix Yarn Company
7 South Tracy Avenue, Bozeman, Montana 59715
406-556-5786
www.stixyarn.com

The Yarn Tree
347 Bedford Avenue
Brooklyn, New York 11211
718-384-8030
info@theyarntree.com, www.theyarntree.com

Shows & Festivals:
- Fiberfest EUREKA, Eureka, Montana

Goat Knoll Farm

Paul Johnson and Linda Fox
2280 S. Church Road, Dallas, Oregon 97338
503-623-8575
goatknoll@fibergoat.com, www.wvi.com/~goatknol

Shows & Festivals:
- Black Sheep Gathering, Lane County Fairgrounds, Eugene, Oregon
- Oregon Flock and Fiber Festival, Clackamas County Fairgrounds, Canby, Oregon
- Sheep to Shawl Festival, Mission Mill, Salem, Oregon

Old Mill Farm

Barbara Sochacki
Cas Sochacki
PO Box 553, Mendocino, California 95460
707-937-3047
barbara@oldmillfarm.org, www.oldmillfarm.org

Old Mill Farm sells its wool directly on the Internet.

Retail Sources:
Mendocino Yarn Shop
PO Box 2475, Mendocino, California 95460
707-937-0921
yarnshop@mcn.org, www.mendocinoyarnshop.com

Mendocino Farmers' Markets in Fort Bragg and Mendocino

Yarn Substitutes

Meadowcroft Farm

All Patterns

 Peace Fleece, 70% wool, 30% mohair, worsted-weight yarn, 200 yd (183m), 4 oz (113.5g), www.peacefleece.com

Classic Elite Yarns Waterlily, 100% extra fine merino, 100 yd (91.5m), 2 oz (50g), www.classiceliteyarns.com

Trim for Low Tide Crossover Vee Sweater

 Trim: Habu Textiles, any laceweight, www.habutextiles.com

Tregellys Farm

All Patterns

 Peace Fleece, 70% wool, 30% mohair, worsted-weight yarn, 200 yd (183m), 4 oz (113.5g), www.peacefleece.com

Vickie Howell Collection Rock, 40% soy silk fibers, 30% wool, 30% hemp, 109 yd (99.5m), 2 oz (50g), www.vickiehowell.com

Autumn House Farm

Welsh Traveling Socks

 Fleece Artist Merino Hand-Painted, 100% washable merino wool, fingering-weight yarn, 370 yd (338.5m), 4 oz (113.5g), www.fleeceartist.com

Claudia Hand-Painted, 100% wool, fingering-weight yarn, 175 yd (160m), 1¾ oz (50g), www.claudiaco.com

Cassandra Cardigan

 Peace Fleece, 70% wool, 30% mohair, DK-weight yarn, 350 yd (320m), 4 oz (113.5g), www.peacefleece.com

Rowan Scottish Tweed, 100% new wool, DK-weight yarn, 123 yd (112.5m), 2 oz (50g), www.knitrowan.com

Misty Meadow Icelandics Farm

All Patterns

Louet North America, fiber batts and roving, sold by weight, www.louet.com

Harrisville Wool Fleece, sold by weight, www.harrisville.com

Kai Ranch

All Patterns

 Brown Sheep Burleyspun, 100% wool, bulky yarn, 132 yd (120.5m), 8 oz (227g), www.brownsheep.com

Blue Sky Alpacas, 50% alpaca, 50% wool, Bulky Naturals or Bulky Hand-Dyes yarn, 45 yd (41m), 3½ oz (100g), www.blueskyalpacas.com

Victory Ranch

All Patterns

 Misti Alpaca Worsted, 100% baby alpaca, worsted-weight, 4-ply yarn, 109 yd (99.5m), 2 oz (50g), www.mistialpaca.com

Cascade Dolce, 55% superfine alpaca, 23% silk, 22% wool, 109 yd (99.5m), 2 oz (50g), www.cascadeyarns.com

Lazy J Diamond Ranch

Hard Rock Snowboarder Sweater

 Brown Sheep Lamb's Pride, 85% wool, 15% mohair, bulky yarn, 125 yd (114.5m), 4 oz (113.5g), www.brownsheep.com

Malabrigo, 100% merino wool, hand-dyed, chunky yarn, 104 yd (95m), 3½ oz (99g), www.malabrigoyarn.com

Navajo Braided Rope
Roving

 Louet North America, fiber batts and roving, sold by weight www.louet.com/

Thirteen Mile Farm

Montana Tunic

 Cascade 220 Heathers Fiber, 100% Peruvian highland wool, 220 yd (201m), 3½ oz (100g), www.cascadeyarns.com

Rowan Scottish Tweed, 100% wool, DK-weight yarn, 123 yd (112.5m), 2 oz (50g), www.knitrowan.com

Lars's Vest

 Peace Fleece, 70% wool, 30% mohair, worsted-weight yarn, 200 yd (183m), 4 oz (113.5g), www.peacefleece.com

Cascade Eco Wool, 100% natural Peruvian wool yarn, 478 yd (437m), 9 oz (250g), www.cascadeyarns.com

Wolf Pack Hat

 Dale of Norway Heilo, 100% wool, sportweight yarn, 109 yd (99.5m), 1¾ oz (49.5g), www2.dale.no

Brown Sheep Nature Spun, 100% wool, sportweight yarn, 184 yd (168m), 1¾ oz (49.5g), www.brownsheep.com

Goat Knoll

Luna Lace Scarf

 Habu Cashmere A-34 2/26, 100% cashmere yarn, 404 yd (369.5m), 1 oz (28g), www.habutextiles.com

Jade Sapphire Mongolian Cashmere, 100% cashmere, 2-ply yarn, 400 yd (366m), 2 oz (55g), www.jadesapphire.com

Worf's Cashmere Socks

 Jade Sapphire Mongolian Cashmere, 100% cashmere, 4-ply yarn, 200 yd (183m), 2 oz (55g), www.jadesapphire.com

Old Mill Farm

All Patterns

 Peace Fleece, 70% wool, 30% mohair, worsted-weight yarn, 200 yd (183m), 4 oz (113.5g), www.peacefleece.com

Cascade Eco Wool, 100% natural Peruvian wool yarn, 478 yd (437m), 9 oz (250g), www.cascadeyarns.com

Standard Yarn Weight System

Categories of yarn, gauge ranges, and recommended needle and hook sizes

Yarn Weight Symbol & Category Names	1 SUPER FINE	2 FINE	3 LIGHT	4 MEDIUM	5 BULKY	6 SUPER BULKY
Type of Yarns in Category	Sock, Fingering, Baby	Sport, Baby	DK, Light Worsted	Worsted, Afghan, Aran	Chunky, Craft, Rug	Bulky, Roving
Knit Gauge Range* in Stockinette Stitch to 4 inches	27–32 sts	23–26 sts	21–24 sts	16–20 sts	12–15 sts	6–11 sts
Recommended Needle in Metric Size Range	2.25–3.25 mm	3.25–3.75 mm	3.75–4.5 mm	4.5–5.5 mm	5.5–8 mm	8 mm and larger
Recommended Needle in U.S. Size Range	1 to 3	3 to 5	5 to 7	7 to 9	9 to 11	11 and larger
Crochet Gauge* Ranges in Single Crochet to 4 inches	21–32 sts	16–20 sts	12–17 sts	11–14 sts	8–11 sts	5–9 sts
Recommended Hook in Metric Size Range	2.25–3.5 mm	3.5–4.5 mm	4.5–5.5 mm	5.5–6.5 mm	6.5–9 mm	9 mm and larger
Recommended Hook in U.S. Size Range	B-1 to E-4	E-4 to 7	7 to I-9	I-9 to K-10 ½	K-10 ½ to M-13	M-13 and larger

Guidelines only: The above reflect the most commonly used gauges and needle or hook sizes for specific yarn categories.

Acknowledgments

Grateful appreciation to Rebecca Davison and Linda Mirabile of RavenMark — who have done all the set-up, the follow-through, the negotiating, the editorial cleanup, the design and production, and the liaison work with great energy and remarkable good cheer. We thank them for the leap of faith for this crazy idea, and for having their year overtaken by sheep, goats, alpaca, and knitting lingo.

And to the farmers and ranchers for their generosity in opening their homes, spending hours answering questions about their lives, demonstrating what they do, and sharing memorable meals:

Jay Begay Jr.
Jody & Ed Cothey
Linda Fox & Paul Johnson
Nanney Kennedy
Harriet & Ken Knox
Judy & Tom McDowell
Jody McKenzie
Lisa & Randy Shell
Barbara & Ben Sochacki
Cas Sochacki
Becky Weed & Dave Tyler
Carol & Ken Weisner
Darcy Weisner

Thanks to other craftspeople, models, designers, and farm and ranch workers who enriched the interviews, stories, photography, and patterns, provided shelter, lent us photo locations, posed with good humor, and made our work so much easier:

Mariposa Archuleta
Molly Baxter
Helen Begay
Michael Begay
John and Laurel Berger
Betty Biggs
Linda, Barry, Sam & Ben Brodsky
Jane & Les Brown
Dean Cheek
Libby & Walt Davis
Victoria Dicken
Kate Dinsmore
Delores Douglass
Brendan Dwyer

Mary Lou Egan
Colin Fissenden
Eileen Fontana
Erica Fox
Sheri Franz
Maryland Grier
Beverly Healy
Lorraine Heasley
Tavi Hillesland
Elaine Wing & Eric Hillesland,
    Alegria Inn, Mendocino
Ann Hovey
Miriam Jacobs
Jeremy Johnson
Annelle Karlstad/Mendocino Yarn Shop
Karen Kassap
Louanne Kirkman
Elizabeth Krause
Anne Lando
Agathe McQueston
Kirsten MacKenzie
Jill McCaughna
Emily and Zack McDowell
Christine Mehser
Aileen Mell
Catherine Mlnarik
Karen Moreland
Liz & Sef Murguia
Mary Olson
Jennifer Olsson/Montana Sweater
    Company, Bozeman
Raymond Pacheco
Louis Pacheco
Jerome & Brianna Pacheco
Hanna Peck
Chuck Penich
Nicholas Petti, Mendo Bistro, Fort Bragg
Katey Plymesser
Bill and Jane Quinn
Talia Rendall
Peter Smith
Karin Steinbrueck
Ian Stewart
Dale & Thomas Taylor
Sandy Trimble
Devra Wagner
Leticia & Liana Vigil
Crystal Yazzie
Rena & Sam Yazzie

Sharon Rooney of the Mendocino County Promotional Alliance for suggesting Old Mill Farm.

Julie Fraenkel for her illustrations.

For technical editing, pattern graphics, copy editing, fact checking, proofreading, indexing, pattern interpreting, substitute yarn advice, and unflagging moral support:

Belinda Broaden
Mary Lou Egan
Patsy Fortney
Kay Gardiner
Dee Gray
Carole Julius
Josie Masterson-Glen
Sue McCain
Ann Shayne
Judy Thurlow
Yarn LLC, New Haven, Connecticut

And all of the blog readers/commenters at
    She Shoots Sheep Shots

The wonderful staff at Potter Craft:

Lauren Shakely, Shawna Mullen and Rosy Ngo, who gave us a thumbs-up right away, Mona Michael, Christina Schoen, Erin Slonaker, Melissa Bonventre, and Chi Ling Moy, each of whom contributed her talents to the project.

Thanks to those who traveled along, held reflectors, pitched hay, or herded unruly ewes:

David Engler, Leo Engler-Zucker, Gabe Engler-Zucker, Linda Zucker, Steve Siegel, Hannah Dawes, Chad Bartlett, Heather McLaughlin

Very special thanks to Rita Zucker for her constant support and many talents: from title brainstorming to test knitting, tech editing, and of course, for inspiring Gale's passion for adventure and knitting.

Index

Page numbers in italic type identify pages that contain photographs of, but notext on, the subject.